THE MONEY SPIDERS

The Ruin-NATION of the United States
by the Federal Reserve

By JP McCarthy

Federal Reserve Note (FRN)

ClearView Press, Inc.
Post Office Box 353431
Palm Coast, FL 32135-3431

ISBN: 978-1-935795-04-9 (soft cover)
ISBN: 978-1-935795-06-3 (Adobe ebook edition)
ISBN: 978-1-935795-05-6 (Amazon Kindle)

LCCN: 201245063

PRINTED IN THE UNITED STATES OF AMERICA

AGES OF DECEIT

Money Changers and Their Schemes
Ages of Deceit and Dirty Themes
Granite Columns Built Just Right
Pure and Solid Hiding Fright
Enriching Themselves Behind Closed Doors
Printing Paper to Make Us Poor

-JP McCarthy, 2008

DEDICATION

This book is dedicated to the memory and patriotism of presidents' Thomas Jefferson and Andrew Jackson. Without their inspiration and words, I would not have written this book. They knew the evils of central banking and throughout their careers they dedicated themselves to the abolishment of having central bankers control the people's money supply. It's my hope that my readers will develop the same feelings and furor that Jefferson and Jackson had against the central bankers.

I also would like to give kudos to the people that have gone before me and to their excellent books explaining the inner workings of the Federal Reserve. To authors G. Edward Griffin, Eustace Clarence Mullins, Rep. Ron Paul and Mike Kirchubel— without your words and inspiration, this book would not be possible. Through your written word, I have seen the light and know the truth. Thank you for setting me free!

JP McCarthy, 2012

TABLE OF CONTENTS

TABLE OF CONTENTS (cont'd)

ACKNOWLEDGEMENTS

When one strikes out on writing any book, it takes a lot of time and effort. In 2006, when I started to investigate the operations of the Federal Reserve, at first, I did it for my own interest/knowledge, but as I got further into the intricacies and fallacies of our central bank, the more time I spent on the subject.

With the above in mind, I would like to thank my immediate family, especially my wife Gina, for her patience in giving me the time to write this book. Without her love and support this book would be in the slush pile in my office. I would also like to thank the following people for their special interest and support: Jason Morrow, Rosemary Beecham, Bob Moynihan, Patricia McCarthy Kelley, Kathy & John Higgs and Patrick McCarthy and Nick Riegel of ITpedia Solutions, for his support as my Webmaster.

Without a publisher, who believes in your work, books don't get professionally published. Many thanks to ClearView Press Inc. Publisher/Editor Michael Ray King and his trustworthy assistant and lovely wife, Bobbie King for their perseverance and hard work in helping me polish this book and get my message out. Without their input, support and influence, this book would not have come to fruition.

Most important, I give thanks to my Creator for providing the knowledge, strength and fortitude to tell my story and helping me realize that He above all else is the Master of the Universe and the driving force behind the founding and salvation of this great country.

THANK YOU!!
JP McCarthy

INTRODUCTION

WHY SHOULD YOU CARE?

The Declaration of Independence, July 4th, 1776

When in the Course of human events, it becomes necessary for one people to dissolve the political bands which have connected them with another, and to assume among the powers of the earth, the separate and equal station to which the Laws of Nature and of Nature's God entitle them, a decent respect to the opinions of mankind requires that they should declare the causes which impel them to the separation.

We hold these truths to be self-evident, that all men are created equal, that they are endowed by their Creator with certain unalienable Rights, that among these are Life, Liberty and the pursuit of Happiness. . .

The above words are immortal and a testament to man's desire to be ruled, not by tyranny, but by *Natural Laws* in communion with *God's Laws*.

This book has been written several times in thought and on paper, searching for the words and theme that would explain the forces that are tearing this great country apart. If one believes in Divine Providence, like our Founding Fathers, then the question would be: What would Jesus want us to do? As I pondered this question, my thoughts turned to the Bible and the answer came clear to me. Jesus sees the deceit and corruption in our money system and would cast out the Money Changers, just like He did in the Gospel according to Matthew in the New Testament. "We the People" need to do the same and it starts at the top with the Money Power, the Federal Reserve.

What follows is a brief history of money and a legal case against the Federal Reserve Banking System. Although, I'm not a lawyer, I see injustice being perpetrated against the American people by the Federal Reserve. They need to be brought to court and exposed. When all is said and done, I pose a question as to whether our central bank is a viable institution or a hindrance to the sovereignty and goodness of the United States. As jury, you will provide the answer. At times my anger towards our banking system shows, knowing the iniquity that has occurred to this great nation since the inception of the Federal Reserve in 1913. As you will see, I feel my rants and rage against the FED are justified.

I offer several obvious and personal solutions to correcting the problems in our banking establishment. These explications are born out of *Natural Law* by taking an unfair and deceitful money system and simply exercising *Common Sense*. This principle of applying simple reason to complex political, social, and money issues is lacking and an obstacle in resolving the problems facing this nation and the world.

Understand, the solutions presented will never take place unless Americans turn to the spiritual laws that govern human nature. Our Founding Fathers knew best. This country was founded on Christian-Judeo principles. Our early politicians infused religious dogma into the American experience that espoused the nature of man and his relationship to God. They relied on Divine Providence and the Bible to guide them in the creation of the United States of America. They understood *"American*

Exceptionalism" before it became popular and a part of the American landscape.

As a country, we need to return to our Founding Fathers and the "Spirit" of 1776. We need to interweave our natural and spiritual sides before this country can heal and be a force in the world once again. From the musical play, *1776*, Andrew McNair, the custodian for the Continental Congress during the deliberations and writing of the Declaration of Independence would exclaim, "Sweet Jesus!" when attending to the needs of our early politicians. We need a little of that sweetness today to right the ship and get it back on course.

Similar to the unfairness of England's King George III towards the Colonies before 1776, we are being treated unjustly by the powerful few and must declare independence from their greed and corruption. But first, look inward and take responsibility for yourself. The U.S. federal government is not the answer to solving our problems.

Despite the dangers and uncertainty, our Founding Fathers signed the Declaration of Independence, knowing their signatures foretold a death sentence. They believed in a deity greater than themselves. Like our Founding Fathers, Americans need the same conviction, fortitude, courage and divinity to "right the wrong" and re-establish the United States as a beacon of freedom throughout the world. Now is the time to renew and restore this great Nation.

"It is the duty of all nations to acknowledge the providence of Almighty God, to obey His will, to be grateful for His benefits, and humbly to implore His protection and favor."

-George Washington, 1st President of the United States
Thanksgiving Proclamation, October 3, 1789

"Sneaky and underhanded, the Federal Reserve has been sucking the life blood out of the United States since 1913. Like a black widow spider, it weaves a web of corruption and deceit. Unknown to its prey, the FED's bite is poisonous, deep, long-lasting and brings financial upheaval and misery to Americans."

-JP McCarthy, 2012

I. THE INDICTMENT

What follows is a direct indictment against the Federal Reserve Banking System. I charge the Federal Reserve with high crimes against the people of the United States. The evidence speaks for itself . . .

Money = POWER

Have you wondered why mainstream media, both liberal and conservative, never tell you the real reason for problems with our economy? Do they ever mention the actual cause of why we have periods of prosperity, followed by bouts of economic recessions and depressions? They give lots of reasons, but never tell us the main cause. Their usual answer is, well, "it's just part of the business cycle." What does that mean? Most pundits and talking heads eagerly remain subservient to the "Money Changers."

Central Bankers Control Our Money,
Our Government & Us!

With the above in mind, the quickest way to clean up Washington D.C. is to take out the Money Power. Like Jesus, we need to banish the Money Changers from the Temple. Forget what you hear from the President and Congressional politicians about debt ceilings, balancing the budget and reducing the National Debt. Until we eliminate the powerful few who control our money, nothing will change – the status quo will always reign supreme.

Popular newscasters and radio show hosts, depending on their political persuasion, present diametric views and opinions. Where does the truth lie? If the media told the truth, most talking heads would lose their jobs. I feel the major media and the ones in control of the financial strings conspire to pull the wool over our eyes. Keeping us guessing, feeds our confusion... and their salaries.

This media disorientation reminds me of lyrics from a STYX song entitled, *Borrowed Time*:

"The Left say Yes and the Right says No
I'm in between and the more I learn,
Well, the less that I know"

Dennis De Young & Tommy Shaw, 1979

Later in the song, *Borrowed Time*, De Young and Shaw switch the "yes and no, to say "no and yes". We are bombarded constantly with opposing views from the media, adding delusion and chaos to our lives. It's no wonder that many Americans have dropped out of the political process and have become apathetic to change and a better life.

Unfortunately, we are pawns in their privileged games and it starts with the financial players and media moguls at the top of the money chain. We are told half-truths and only what they want us to hear. If we knew the other half . . . God help us. *Control* is the name of the game.

The following pages are not fairy tales written to amuse you. In fact, it will infuriate and disgust you. I've based this book on factual information and when I inject my personal opinion, like the above, I will tell you. With that said, please don't take what you are about to read as hard facts. As I did, when I first started this inquiry, I said, *"No way . . . this can't be true! . . . Why has our government sold out to private bankers?* As I read and gathered more information, it came to me that we live in an artificial world, controlled by forces that hide in plain view. Like a snake in the grass, the truth is elusive and hard to grasp. If you've seen the movie, *The Matrix*, you know what I'm talking about. You need to do your own due diligence and find out the truth for yourself. Only then will you be convinced of this altered world we live in.

In the early 70's, Gloria Steinem, of the Feminist Movement, said, *"The truth will set you free. But first, it will piss you off."* I suspect that most of you will have a fit once you understand how our banking system works against us and what it has done to destroy you and this great country.

My hope is this book will give you the grounding and impetus to do further research and arrive at the same conclusion that I have . . . *that we are indentured servants to the powerful few and through our hard labor they make tons of money, keeping us enslaved and in the dark*. I challenge you to acquire information you will never hear on TV, read in the newspapers or discuss on talk radio. Why? The Money Power, with the support of the major media, keeps us from the truth so they can continue to work their black magic. A simple axiom of human behavior is when people are confused and don't understand, they are easier to control.

Before ever thinking about writing a simple approach to understanding the complicated Federal Reserve, I took it upon myself to read as much as I could about the workings of our central bank. Please know that there have been several excellent books written on the Federal Reserve (see bibliog.). Of the books I've read, two are remarkable resources:

1. *The Creature from Jekyll Island* by G. Edward Griffin (reads like a history book)

2. *A Study of the Federal Reserve and its Secrets* by Eustace Mullins (lots of dates & names)

Both books offer an outstanding insight into what makes the FED tick and how it has been destructive to the welfare of this country and to American citizens in particular. I encourage you to read both books and supplement your knowledge in addition to what you will learn from the pages of this book. Griffin's and Mullin's books are great references and handy when one needs in-depth information about the FED. Both have a tendency to get lost in details with lots of dates and name-dropping. Although Griffin's book is a must read, I do have disagreements on his solutions to ending the Federal Reserve. We need to take the power away from the FED and we do that in little steps by creating our own money instead of borrowing it.

The main purpose of this book is to explain in simple terms what all Americans should know about the Federal Reserve and our money system. I feel that the FED purposely makes our money system appear mysterious with smoke and mirrors to fool and distort. They use fancy phrases, like, *Quantitative Easing* (QE) to keep us confused and clueless. QE is nothing more than the Federal Reserve buying government debt (T-bills) and infusing more fake money into the financial system. This action has a disastrous affect on cheapening our dollar and causing inflation. What follows is a clear, concise course on the Federal Reserve that I've tried to keep factual, hard-hitting, to the point and understandable.

It is my sincere hope that this book will throw a bright, informative light on the "FED" and instill a sense of wonderment, coupled with revulsion. With that, I also believe that Knowledge = POWER and hope this information will stir your emotions, while emitting a call for action. A bit of caution – *if you have knowledge and don't use it or take* <u>*action*</u>*, then knowledge is worthless.*

Quite frankly, "We the People" need to take back this country from the powerful few. Nothing will change, I mean *NOTHING*, until we abolish the Federal Reserve and start *CREATING* our own money.

Are you ready to learn how your money is used against you and why we have economic turmoil? We are about to embark on an eye-opening journey that at times will blow your mind and question the very foundation, soul and principles of this great country. Hold on to your seat, you are in for a rough ride, but an exciting awakening.

"I care not what puppet is placed upon the throne of England to rule the Empire . . . The man that controls Britain's money supply controls the British Empire, and I control the British money supply."

-Baron Nathan Mayer Rothschild,
of the Rothschild International Banking Cartel, 1815

I purposely used bold type to help burn this quote into your memory. Rothschild, head of the Bank of England, threatened this country if Congress did not renew the Charter of the 1st Bank of the United States in 1811. Congress defeated the measure by one vote and surprisingly, the U.S. went to war with England the next year. Powerful bankers even back then influenced the course of history! If you substitute the Federal Reserve into the above quote then nothing has changed in over 200 years!

It has been well documented that our Founding Fathers knew about the evils of central banking. They railed against private bankers having control of the money supply of "their" fledgling United States of America. Many saw how King George III bowed to England's central bank, owned by the Rothschild family. They saw how this bank produced "bills of credit" and unjustly, through King George, over taxed the Colonies to support Britain's expanding empire. Many historians feel that the Bank of England, not King George, caused the hostilities between the Colonies and England. These "money" conflicts led to the Revolutionary War and the birth of the United States in 1776. Throughout the writings and deliberations of our Founding Fathers in the Declaration of Independence, the Articles of Confederation, the Constitution and Bill of Rights, numerous speeches and dissertations came out against allowing banks to control the nation's money supply. Without a doubt, history shows that many of our early citizens/politicians wanted our country's economy based on real money that had *intrinsic* value like silver and gold coins. They understood through past experiences and history that once a country starts to debase, then inflate its money, the ones in charge profited, while the common man was pilfered and suffered untold misery. This country was founded on the principle of "We the People" and when private bankers had control of the "people's money" (1st & 2nd Banks of the United States), this founding principle became secondary to the banker's personal gain and a detriment to the people's Freedom and Rights guaranteed by the Constitution. This same scenario is happening today.

Our current central bank, the Federal Reserve, is patterned after Rothschild's Bank of England. Don't let the name fool you. <u>It's NOT Federal, it doesn't have any Reserves and is operated by a group of Rich, Private "Connected" Bankers.</u> Which begs the question . . . *Why do we allow connected bankers to run our money supply?* Isn't it akin to having a fox guard the hen house? If Founding Father, Thomas Jefferson, was alive today he would recognize the deceit, corruption and shenanigans of our central bank. He would see how the Federal Reserve has ransacked the entire house and made a mockery of the U.S. Constitution. The author of our Declaration of Independence throughout his lifetime was vehemently against private bankers controlling our money supply. He understood how central bankers in collusion with the government eroded the People's individual freedom and wealth. The U.S. Government has gotten out of hand with spending to the tune that every taxpayer's share of the National Debt is more than $130,000 and rising. A government this big was not the intentions of our Founding Fathers.

"A government big enough to give you everything you want, is a government big enough to take from you everything you have."

-Gerald R. Ford, 38th U.S. President
Presidential address to Congress, August 12, 1974

This book will give you a short History on money, leading to the Founding of this country, the 1st & 2nd Banks of the United States, Andrew Jackson's victory, Abe Lincoln's Greenbacks and finally the Beginnings of the Federal Reserve and what this Central Bank has done to destroy the Sovereignty of the United States and its people. Finally, we will look at what we can do and the possible Outcomes to Current Events.

I hope you will take this information and share it with your family, friends and spread the word. I would like to see every American holding a copy of this book as they stand outside the Federal Reserve in Washington D.C. with a book in one hand and a fist raised on the other, demanding the FED's abolishment as a black spot on the U.S. Constitution and restoration of the Freedom and Rights of every American.

We possess the numbers to make change, but lack the knowledge. This book picks up the slack, fills the void and connects the dots. Take a few seconds and re-read the opening quote from this chapter. After reading this book, return to this quote. Does it ring true? If so, what are YOU doing about it?

"The rich rule over the poor, and the borrower is servant to the lender"

-Proverbs 22:7

II. THE MONEY GAME

For the sake of discussion, it's important to understand the concept of money. Everyone has their own definition of what money means to them. To understand how our money has been used against us, we need to start with a few definitions. We can't play the money game unless we understand the basics.

WHAT IS MONEY?

As important as money is to people, most of us take it for granted. We treat money as a valuable resource without giving thought to what money really is, where it comes from, or how it works.

Before one can truly understand the Federal Reserve and the evil effects it has had on this country, we need to take a short trip back in history. I will defer to the scholars of ancient cultures to discuss fully the effects of money on civilizations. A belief of many historians is if one follows the money, the truth can be found. For our purpose, the truth starts around the Bronze Age when metals were discovered. Fascinated, man started shaping

> Throughout history money has played a role in historical events.

these shiny pieces of matter into different forms and a new kind of money came into existence called *commodity money*. Precious metals like gold and silver became popular as commodity money because both are limited in nature, can be stored easily and measured – qualities that, as you will see, are important in any honest money system. Being able to "measure" a quantity of gold, for example, an ounce, allowed this metal to function very nicely as a "storehouse of value." In other words, *"it is what it is"* and only man can change it by manipulating its set measure.

When the United States Mint came into operation in Philadelphia in 1792, it produced gold and silver coins that had specific weights and measures, giving validity and peace of mind to early Americans when used in trade and commerce. Do we have that today?

First, understand that money is anything which is accepted as a *medium of exchange*. If we accept this definition then anything that has value to the people transacting the exchange can be used as money. The key word is *VALUE*. Without having value as determined by the parties involved, then the transaction would not take place, consequently, a nation's commerce would be severely limited.

If my country's medium for exchange were bananas of uniform shape and weight, then based on the "agreed value" of bananas, goods and services could be traded for a corresponding amount of bananas. Of course, bananas would never be used as money due to spoilage and storage problems. Let's say, I give you two bananas to paint my house. We both recognize the value of bananas and agree on the payment for your labor and supplies to paint my house. We do the deal and shake hands on it. We just used bananas as a medium of exchange or money.

Our money today has NO value and the only reason it exists is due to *legal tender laws* which forces us and merchants to use and accept money in exchange for goods and services. American citizens can be fined and put in the locker for refusing to accept *Federal Reserve Notes* (FRN's). FRN's are just pieces of paper with no precious metal backing or value. The fake money that the FED makes out of nothing is money that isn't even worth the paper it's printed on! If we used real money like gold and silver coins to do business and Uncle Sam caught wind of it, we could be subject to fines and possibly thrown in jail. What kind of justice is that!

Real Money versus Fake Money

Ever since 1933, when the U.S. government under President Franklin Roosevelt confiscated the people's gold, we have been beholding to the Federal Reserve and gone deeper and deeper into debt. The National Debt is at astronomical numbers and rising by the second. We are a debtor nation caused by the continued manipulation and debasement of our money, courtesy of the Federal Reserve. The dollar bill in your purse or wallet is not worth the paper it's printed on. Our dollar has lost over 95% of its value since the Federal Reserve Act of 1913 (see Appendix). In 1912, I could exchange a dollar's worth of goods and services for $1. Today that same dollar only purchases less than five cents of goods and services. How did this happen? Before the Federal Reserve, Americans used silver and gold coins in their daily commerce. Where did all of those silver and gold coins go? What happened to that distinct sound and weight of real money jiggling in our forefather's pockets? How did the dollar lose its value? The paper money that is issued by our central bank today is an illusion. It doesn't have intrinsic value. Intrinsic value (IV) is an important concept to remember. This fake money – the Federal Reserve Notes (FRNs) that you are now using are worth nothing. They are made out of thin air with the stroke of keyboard. The only reason FRN's are viable as an exchanged medium is that the Federal government requires merchants, employers, contractors et al, to accept them to satisfy a debt. The only real money we have in circulation today is the pocket change we carry. This money is at least worth the cheap base metals that the U.S. Mint uses to produce it. Incidentally, only 3% of our money circulates as Federal Reserve Notes, the rest exist as computer digits. How fake can that be?

Conversely, silver and gold coins have intrinsic value. See Spanish Silver Pillar Dollar, on left. This money is real, based on the value of the precious silver contained within. For example, around 1900 anyone could go to a local bank and offer five silver $1 coins (Morgan Dollars) and receive in return a $5 dollar paper silver certificate.

$5 PAPER SILVER CERTIFICATE 1899

During this time, our money was backed by "intrinsic-valued" precious metals. Our money had substance and value. Both paper certificates and silver/gold coins were used in commerce to satisfy debts. Today, if you attempted to exchange that five dollar Lincoln Federal Reserve Note for five silver dollar coins, the bank teller would laugh you out of the bank.

If you ever played the game *Monopoly*, and controlled the bank, what did you do when other players couldn't pay their way? Ever hear of foreclosure? Maybe you have been "foreclosed" on? Banks do that whether the economy is up or down. The confiscation of property through foreclosures is a form of thievery, supported by our government and the monetary policies of our Federal Reserve. What other forms of theft has our central bank committed against the American people in its almost 100 years of existence? Plenty! But first, let's see how money has played a role in history and the formation of this country.

Ready, get set . . . *GO...OO.* Don't forget to collect your fake $200.00 in Federal Reserve Notes when you pass go!

"My people are destroyed from lack of knowledge . . ."

-Hosea 4:6

III. In the Beginning . . .
The Money Changers

There have been many civilizations who have come and gone and have used different exchange mediums. Ancient Greece had a good run with their gold drachma *coinage for several centuries. Ancient Greece's successful, enlightened leadership in the world was based on its honest money system. One group of people, the Byzantines, stands out as a bright light against a dark sky concerning money matters. No people or civilization, either ancient or modern, has ever reached the zenith the Byzantines accomplished in their handling and operation of its money supply. The Byzantine Empire survived and prospered for over 700 years, without ever debasing its money or going into debt. The mainstay of their money system was a gold coin called a* bezant. *This coin was accepted throughout the land due to its consistent value and the fact that it could be measured. People thrived based on a reliable money supply that wasn't controlled or manipulated by a king, dictator or central bank.*

> Any time an honest money system based on intrinsic value was in place the people prospered.

Let's look at some examples of events in history where money played a key role in the outcome.

Julius Caesar

Brutus and Cassius assassinated Julius Caesar in 44 B.C. What history books don't tell you is that Caesar figured out that when the Money Changers were in control of the Empire's money, they controlled the government and its people, especially Caesar's soldiers. Back in those days if a soldier didn't get paid in a timely manner, there would be widespread mutiny and unrest – not conducive to Rome's expanding borders. Caesar started to produce his own money (silver & gold coins), and the country experienced several years of prosperity, growth and good fortune, much to the dismay of the Money Changers. Alas, after much court intrigue and (excuse the pun) "back-stabbing," Caesar was eliminated and his successful money system destroyed and replaced by the Money Changer's schemes.

Some historians feel that Caesar's murder was the start of the "Fall of Rome." By 300 A.D. Rome was in tailspin with extended borders, mutiny in the army, an empty treasury, agriculture that seemed non-existent and trade at a standstill. The United States is heading in a similar direction with porous, undefined borders, an overextended military, farming in decline and a country on the edge of bankruptcy.

The Roman Empire never recovered. By the 7th century money became extinct and the Roman Empire ceased to exist.

Cleansing of the Temple

In a biblical story that is well known, Jesus had to use force to stop the Money Changer's deceit and corruption. He saw the greed demonstrated by the Money Changers when they cornered the market on the Jewish half-shekel. This silver coin was highly sought due to its purity and measured weight. The Money Changers saw they could corner the market then hoarded and inflated the *half-shekel* causing the Jewish people to pay more in Temple taxes. Jesus saw this injustice to His people and cast the "Den of Thieves" out of the Temple.

"And Jesus went into the temple of God, and cast out all them that sold and bought in the temple, and overthrew the tables of the moneychangers, and the seats of them that sold doves, and said unto them, "It is written, my house shall be called the house of prayer, but ye have made it a den of thieves."

-Matthew 21:12-13 KJV

This wasn't the first time, or last, that Money Changers (bankers) have been called a Den of Thieves. It happened again in the 1830's in this country with Andrew Jackson, but more on that later. For the record, and according to scripture, this was one of the few times that Jesus ever used anger to make a point in his ministry.

Talley-Sticks of Merry Ole England

In the middle ages, man devised an ingenious way of keeping track of who owed what to whom - enter the wooden Talley-Stick. Discussing this simple, but

> Starting in 1100 A.D., Talley-Sticks were used as a form of record and money.

effective medium of exchange is a great example that anything can exist as "money" as long as it's accepted, honest and can be measured. During this time, there was a constant shortage of money (coins), coupled with wide-spread illiteracy. Something needed to be designed to record bilateral exchange and debts. Society and commerce were in dire need of a good measuring device. Without something of value to use in the exchange of goods and services, chaos and anarchy would exist. The Talley-Stick consisted of a piece of squared Hazelwood that was split down the middle with notches added. The number of notches, their location and how they fit together determined the value of the "stick." One of the refinements was to make the two halves of the stick of different lengths. The longer part was called the *stock* and was given to the party which had advanced the money or item to the receiver. The shorter portion of the stick was called the *foil* and was given to the party which had received the funds or goods. By using this technique each of the parties had an identifiable record of the transaction.

The most prominent and best recorded use of the "split" tally stick as a form of currency was when King Henry I initiated the tally stick system around 1100 in medieval England. The King carved an assortment of notches on the stick representing different values. This system of money continued in use for 726 years, ending in 1826.

It's interesting to note that pieces of wood had more value and a consistent purpose in history than the worthless pieces of paper money created out of thin air by the Federal Reserve.

Goldsmiths

> Goldsmiths around the 15th century were the first bankers who developed the concept of fractional banking.

Around the 15th century, craftsmen known as goldsmiths started to store their customer's gold and silver. They already had their own vaults and storage areas, so the next logical step would be to start accepting precious metals from others and charge a nominal fee. At first, a customer would deposit his gold pieces and get a receipt. The receipt or certificate indicated the amount which could be redeemed at anytime. Bingo, the profession of banking came into being. The first IOU's were so popular, that the people started to exchange them among themselves and the checking industry was born. People wrote out a modified IOU (check), handed it to the merchant and he took it to the goldsmith to exchange it for money in gold or silver. This system worked well for many years until the goldsmiths figured out a way to con their clients and buyers by giving out more and more receipts, without covering the amount they received in precious metals (their reserves). In other words, lending gold and silver on credit or advancing more money than he had in his vault. Presto, a process called *Fractional Reserve Banking* came to the forefront.

Banks today use fractional reserve banking to create money out of nothing. They lend money to you, while keeping only a "fraction" of the bank's reserves on the books to cover their bank deposits and loans. This type of banking is another form of thievery supported by our government and the Federal Reserve. To restore honesty in our banking system, financial institutions should be required to keep on hand 100% of what money they lend. If a million dollars are lent, then the bank should have a million dollars in reserve. Understand that if there is a "run on the bank" when people demand their money all at once, fractional reserve banking fails miserably and causes anger, confusion and financial problems. Oh, but wait, you say "The FDIC (Federal Deposit Insurance Corporation) will cover my money if my bank goes belly-up, right?" . . . It also snows in hell! In my opinion, the FDIC is another fraud perpetuated on the American people by the FED and our government.

BANK OF ENGLAND

In the above example with the goldsmiths, the depositors caught wind of the scheme, ran the bank, and demanded a better system. The Bank of England (above) came to the rescue around the turn of the 17th century (1694).

The Bank of England promised to operate a more efficient and honest system, but only made the monetary affairs of the people worse. As has been the case numerous times in history, bankers promise the money supply is in good hands, but turn the tables on the people by lining their own pockets while hiding behind the guise of "your money is safe with us."

The Federal Reserve Banking System is very much like the goldsmiths of the 15th/16th century, the only difference is their deceit and corruption is on a much larger scale and sanctioned by the U.S. government.

Bullet Points to Remember

- throughout history money has played a role in historical events

- money can be anything of agreed value that is used as a medium of exchange

- anytime an honest money system based on intrinsic value was in place, the people prospered; Ancient Greece and Byzantine Empire were prime examples of honest money being used in commerce

- the Byzantines are the only nation in history who never debased their money or went into debt based on a gold coin (unit of measurement) called the Bezant

- starting in 1100 A.D., Talley-Sticks were used as a form of money/record in England for over 700 years and proves the point that anything can be used as a medium of exchange if the parties involved accept the measured value

- Goldsmiths around the 15th century were the first bankers who developed the concept of fractional banking by lending out more of their reserves than they had in their vaults and charging interest; deposits and checking concepts came into being

- the Bank of England was established in 1694

<u>Key Questions to Ponder</u>

1. What is Money?

2. How did Banking start?

3. What constitutes an Honest Money System?

4. How did the goldsmiths con their customers?

5. Why did the ancient Greek and Byzantine Empires prosper?

"That is simple. In the Colonies we issue our own money. It is called Colonial Scrip. We issue it in proper proportion to the demands of trade and industry to make the products pass easily from the producers to the consumers. In this manner, creating for ourselves our own paper money, we control its purchasing power, and we have no interest to pay no one."

-Benjamin Franklin, 1763, explaining to the Bank of England his ideas on why the Colonies were so prosperous.

IV. The Birth of a Nation & the Debt Game

Colonial Scrip

BENJAMIN FRANKLIN

The old Sage knew what he was talking about! The above quote from Mr. Franklin is wordy, a great example of his wit and wisdom. In these words, he sums up what most future Founding Fathers, especially Thomas Jefferson, felt about private bankers producing and safeguarding the "We the People's" money. Read the words, *CREATING* for ourselves our *OWN* paper money, we *CONTROL* its purchasing power and we have no *INTEREST* to pay no one." Today, our money is borrowed, we have no control over it, don't own it and we pay interest on every dollar printed. Take a minute and think carefully what those four words mean in the context of how our money is handled and produced today by the Federal Reserve. Read Ben's quote again.

By the turn of the 17th century, most colonies had their own scrip. The scrip money system worked well for the Colonies and prosperity prevailed with full employment, no income tax and price stability. In harmony with

> The first colony to produce paper money was Massachusetts in 1690.

scrip money, the colonies used Spanish and Portuguese gold and silver coins (Pieces of Eight, America's First Dollar - see below) in their daily commerce, which added to the stable economy, promoting a general feeling of good-will. This tranquility amongst the Colonies all changed when England started to enact Currency Laws, taking away the Colonies power to "create" their own money. The Bank of England realized that Colonial Scrip was affecting their bottom line and petitioned the English Parliament to pass the Currency Act of 1764. Apparently, the British Parliament cared more about the Bank of England's needs than their kindred brethren across the pond. The Currency Law passed and the colonists were forced to borrow all of their money from the Bank of England and pay them interest. Once the greedy bankers got their dirty hands into the pockets of the colonists, all hell broke loose! With the loss of scrip and less money available, an economic depression took place. Many historians believe that the Currency Laws imposed on the colonists were the main reason they revolted against "Tyrant" King George III. Instead of being able to create their own money, now the colonists had to go through England's central

bank and borrow their money from private bankers, at interest, no less! Many feel that the Bank of England caused the fight for independence in 1776, leading to the United States of America. From my perspective, the tax on tea was a minor issue.

1ST SILVER DOLLAR

> The first silver dollar used in America's thirteen original states was a Spanish dollar that was minted at the oldest mints of the New World. Mexico, Peru, Bolivia, Guatemala, and Chile were among the countries that produced this treasured coin. Recommended as the official coinage for the new United States of America by Thomas Jefferson, this coin was the basic currency of our Founding Fathers, widely circulated during the post-Revolutionary era and used as legal tender until 1857. When it was first introduced, it replaced another Spanish silver dollar, known as the "pillar dollar," which had been used by colonists for decades.
>
> The "piece of eight," as this coin is often called, had a value of 8 *reales*. Merchants would sometimes break the coin into eight pieces, each commonly known as "a bit," allowing for purchases of other than whole dollar amounts. English-speakers were the first to refer to this coin as a "dollar." Many experts believe that the pillar and scroll design on the coin's reverse inspired the U.S. dollar sign. The design on the obverse of the coin features the King of Spain, which is why the coin is also known as the "portrait dollar."
>
> The "piece of eight" was a leading medium of international trade. It found its way into the coffers of merchants in Europe and Asia. Small marks, most of which are Chinese symbols, are evident on many specimens indicating that the merchant tested the silver content and stamped his seal of approval directly into the coin.

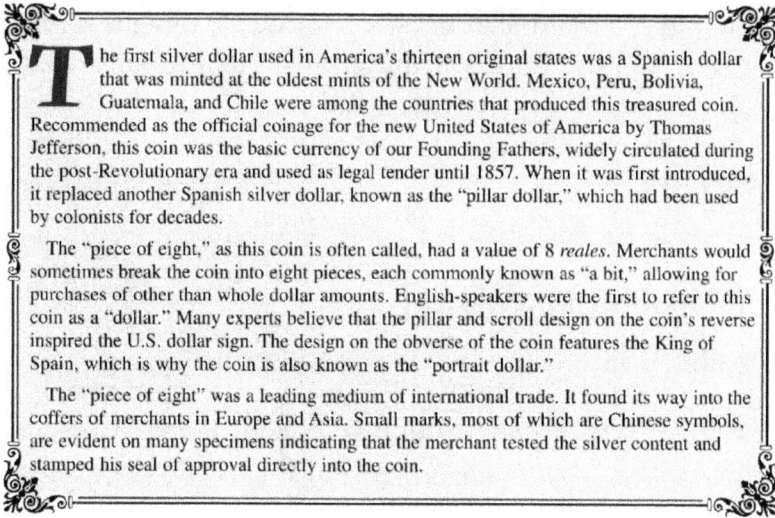

Author, Eustace Mullins in his book, <u>The World Order</u>, 1985, page 31, sums up how the monetary policies of the Bank of England led to the Revolutionary War;

"The Bank of England has played a prominent role in American history – without it, the United States would not exist. The American colonists considered themselves loyal Englishmen to a man, but when they began to enjoy unequalled prosperity by printing and circulating their own Colonial scrip, the stockholders of the Bank of England went to George III and informed him that their monopoly of interest-bearing notes in the colonies was at stake. He banned the scrip, with the result that there was an immediate depression in the commercial life of the Americas. This was the cause of the Rebellion; as Benjamin Franklin pointed out, the little tax on tea, amounting to about a dollar a year per American family, could have been borne, but the colonists could not survive the banning of their own money."

Throughout the history of the U.S., private central bankers have deceived the American people for their own profit by charging interest on borrowed money. Is it a surprise that our Federal Reserve is patterned after England's central bank? Even today, the Bank of England has a direct influence on the American people. As we will find out, the private central bankers are all inter-connected on an international level, causing chaos in economies around the world. And guess what? . . . When you lose, they win.

> The U.S. Constitution specifically states that Congress would coin money and set the standard measures.

Not Worth a Continental

When the colonists had enough of "purchasing" their money from the Bank of England, they opted for freedom and declared their independence from Great Britain. As we all know, the rest is history. But within that history, the Continental Congress struggled and had no choice but to print its own paper money to fund the war with England. At first the paper money was on par with the Spanish silver dollar, but as the war went on the scrip lost its value through excessive printing and counterfeiting by the enemy. By War's end, the saying, *"not worth a continental"* came into vogue and the money that helped forge a nation died a pauper's death. Even George Washington, the Commander of the Continental Army, in a letter to John Jay in April 1779, had these choice words to say about the money, *"A wagon-load of money will scarcely purchase a wagon-load of provisions."*

The Continental paper money would have done better under different circumstances. Remember, when paper money is printed in excess compared to goods and services, inflation runs rampant. The combination of counterfeiting (good tactic by the British) and excessive printing caused the Continental to lose its value through inflation to the point of becoming worthless. Does this sound familiar? Isn't this what is happening today with our Federal Reserve? The FED's printing of excessive dollars until they become worthless. Don't we learn from history? . . . Do we? . . . And guess what? It happens again and again! From the debasement of the Continental, the Founding Fathers understood the pitfalls of having inordinate amounts of paper money in circulation. They were careful and put a provision in the Constitution protecting the people from the excesses of private bankers. In the U.S. Constitution, *Article 1, Section 8,* specifically states that Congress would coin money and set the standard measures. Nothing is said about NOT having a central bank. Where our Founding Fathers went wrong is they never specifically came out against the United States having a central bank. They made the mistake of leaving it wide-open for others to interpret. This oversight would return incessantly to haunt the halls of Congress and the Supreme Court for many years.

I wonder what our Founding Fathers would think about our central bank and the economic issues facing this country today. A multi-trillion dollar National Debt would be incomprehensible to them, as it is to most Americans.

I'm reminded of a Tennessee Ernie Ford song written in the 1950's. Ernie was a radio and TV star during this era and had his own show. I recall his boisterous baritone voice belting out the lyrics which today are poignant reminders of our personal and National Debt. It goes like this:

"You load sixteen tons, what do you get
Another day older and deeper in debt
Saint Peter don't you call me 'cause I can't go
I owe my soul to the company store"

Take one guess who owns the company store?

The Bank of North America (N.A.)

The Bank of North American was the United States first foray into the banking business. The people hoped Canada would come into the new "union" and become a member, hence, the moniker "North America." Chartered by the Continental Congress in 1781 and led by Robert Morris, a member of Congress, this bank essentially modeled itself after the Bank of England. Although not given all the favors associated with a true central bank, Morris ran it like one, practicing fractional banking, which led to excessive paper money and inflation. Riddled with fraud and corruption, the bank lasted for three years failing to have its charter renewed in 1784.

On an interesting note, our Founding Fathers allowed the Bank of N.A. and granted them permission to issue bills of credit. Did they not know that debt money caused problems? We must remember that a war raged at this time and the Continental Congress needed money to fund the hostilities, since by this time the Colonies own scrip proved worthless. Also of note, Morris' protégé, Alexander Hamilton showed himself as a young upstart and eager to learn about the banking business. Hamilton acquired important knowledge through working at the Bank of N.A., which later figured into the creation of the second bank in U.S. history.

The First Bank of the United States

Although titled as "First Bank," in all actuality the creation of this bank in the early 1790's became the second bank of the United States. Led by Federalist, Alexander Hamilton, then Secretary of the Treasury under George Washington, the bank again patterned itself after Rothschild's Bank of England. Why Congress enlisted another bank to "watch and protect" the people's money goes beyond understanding. After the problems with the Continental currency and the Bank of North America, you would think those bad experiences and the U.S. Constitution would trump any notion of having private bankers controlling the nation's money supply. This controversy over centralized banking led to the development of the political parties we have today. Thomas Jefferson and Alexander Hamilton had opposing views about the role of government. Jefferson represented the working class and championed the unconstitutionality of a central bank. Hamilton was a banker and in favor of centralized banking.

In writing about the rift between Hamilton and Jefferson, G. Edward Griffin in his book, The Creature from Jekyll Island p.329, stated that-

Nothing could be more polarized than the opposing ideas of these two men:

Jefferson: *"A private central bank issuing the public currency is a greater menace to the liberties of the people than a standing army. We must not let our rulers load us with perpetual debt."*

ALEXANDER HAMILTON

Hamilton: *"No society could succeed which did not unite the interest and credit of rich individuals with those of the state." A national debt, if it is not excessive, will be to us a national blessing."*

I wonder what Hamilton would say about our National Debt today? Would he consider that excessive? Also, Jefferson predicted and supported throughout his lifetime that the U.S. would be burdened with perpetual debt if private bankers got a hold of the people's money supply. Jefferson knew a thing or two about individual rights and how debt eats away at those rights and ultimately freedom.

The Hamiltonians (Federalist) got around the Constitution by saying the document did not specifically grant the power to create such a bank, but nevertheless, an *implied power* existed. They argued the bank was needed to accomplish other government functions stated in the Constitution. President George Washington sided with Hamilton and the bank was given a 20-year charter. It opened its door in 1791 much to the chagrin of the Jeffersonians. Incidentally, two separate political parties came out of this argument:

1. The Federalist (Republican Party) – wanted a strong central government with more power.

2. The Anti-Federalist (Democratic Party) – wanted a de-centralized government with limited power.

Originally, the Anti-Federalists were known as Jefferson's Republican's, but later morphed into the Democratic Party.

This battle over the legality of a private central bank took on epic proportions over the next 45 years of this country's history. The central bank's constitutional controversy existed until President Andrew Jackson shut down the Banker's Bank for good in 1835.

> The United States existed without a central bank for 78 years. The central bank raised its ugly head again in the early 1900's.

In many economic and political discussions, the central bank question raises the ire of people on both sides of the issue. I only see one issue and that is *a private central bank creating excessive money out of nothing can't be good for the people!* This is exactly what happened in the 20 year existence of the First Bank of the United States. As the United States started to flex its muscle within its borders and around the world, the bank did do some good in fostering commerce. In this respect, the bank met a need at the time, BUT, more problems cropped up than were solved concerning the people's money.

> The most powerful institutions on earth are the world's Central Banks.

History does repeat itself. The bankers got richer as the people got poorer and the bank's charter was not renewed by one vote in the Senate in 1811. Senator Henry Clay cast the deciding vote. Lurking in the background and threatening the United States if the charter was not renewed stood Nathan Rothschild from the Bank of England. What's incredulous is Rothschild owned the bulk of shares in the 1st Bank of the U.S. After his tinkering failed, the United States went to war the next year (1812). Know where there's a war, there's a central banker supporting the conflict. While Rothschild "banked" in England, his brother financed Napoleon. The Rothschild banking family ruled Europe at this time (see Chap. XII, Other Topics, Rothschild's). Nothing has changed. Foreign banking interests are still influential in U.S. political agendas. The international banking community is well connected. Money is power and it talks. Throughout history, this power has affected change in social structure and governments of the world. What's occurring in Europe today is a prime example.

The most powerful institutions on earth are the world's central banks. The international central banking cartel, including our Federal Reserve, through their monetary policies and schemes conspire to own and control us.

An interesting creature developed during the tenure of the First Bank of the United States called *Plutocracy* - a marriage between the wealthy and the government. This arrangement was a government that Jefferson desired to prevent and Hamilton hoped would happen. Both adhered to the philosophy of what they thought was good for the country. This animal is in plain sight, alive today and infecting us daily. Hamilton would be proud of his labor. Jefferson embarrassed by the results.

> Plutocracy is a marriage between the wealthy and the government.

> The 2008 financial collapse was due to an abundance of cheap, easy FED money, supported by the moral hazard syndrome and greed.

A prime example of this happened when two government agents in 2008, named Tim Geithner and Henry Paulson sat in their comfortable chairs and "begged" for taxpayers money to rescue "too big to fail" investment banks on Wall Street. President George Bush capitulated to the bankers; Obama continued the charade and the bankers again used the American people to save their necks and enrich their pockets. These investment banks, supported by the monetary policies of the Federal Reserve, should have failed. The free market, not the government, should have picked up the pieces and restored honesty in our financial system. When a bank or any business makes poor decisions there should be consequences. In the banking industry, financial institutions operate from within a moral hazard, with the invincible feeling of doing anything they want, including dealing in risky investments. They know the taxpayer will pick up the tab if anything goes wrong.

The 2008 financial collapse was due to an abundance of cheap, easy FED money, supported by the moral hazard syndrome and greed. Thanks to Bush in 2008 and Obama in 2009, the poor American taxpayer paid again. This kind of "too big to fail" mentality needs to stop! Unfortunately, most banks are beholding to the top echelon at the Federal Reserve. If honesty in banking held the norm, we would not be in this financial mess and our children would own a decent future.

Hamilton would be proud of the above government officials. They did a great job of *"uniting the interest and credit of rich individuals with those of the state."* It's still going on after 200+ years. But wait, we have only touched the surface of the early U.S. banking history. Put your gas mask on, we have lots of digging to do and it stinks!

The Second Bank of the United States
or the 3rd Central Bank

Nathan Rothschild of the Bank of England stuffed his pockets with blood money when England went to war with the United States in 1812. Remember, he financed England's Napoleonic Wars and made tons of money on that deal with false pretenses and outright thievery. He fooled the London stock market by pretending Wellington's defeat at the Battle of Waterloo in 1815. Stocks went into a selling frenzy and the stock market plunged. Prices collapsed. Rothschild reversed his position and in one quick swoop bought up all of the government bonds and became a dominant holder of England's debt. One of his brothers took the opposite side and financed Napoleon during the Napoleonic Wars with England. These bankers have no scruples when it comes to financing wars as we shall discover after 1913. The House of Rothschild perfected this unholy alliance between government and power-hungry central bankers.

By some historical accounts, after the most unnecessary war in its history, the United States chartered another central bank in 1815. Sinking in debt and reeling from inflation as a result of the War of 1812, Congress sided with the bankers, putting the people's money again in jeopardy with a central bank. I often wonder if Nathan Rothschild had anything to do with America's 3rd central bank. The only reason your scribe could come up with as to why our government established another U.S. central bank is the "special" relationship, excuse me, illicit COLLUSION that central bankers have with politicians. Quite frankly, central bankers and politicians sleep in the same bed with huge smiles on their faces. Time and again, they have used each other to satisfy their agendas at the expense of the American people.

Meanwhile, Jefferson's Democrats kept up the pressure on the bank's unconstitutionality, but got shot down in a monumental Supreme Court case (*McCulloch vs. Maryland*) in 1819. The Chief Justice at this

> The *necessary and proper* clause in the Constitution has been used numerous times since to pass political agendas not supported by what many feel is the original intent of our Constitution.

time was John Marshall, a leading Federalist and supporter of a centralized, powerful federal government. This decision set a precedent for support of a federal central bank. We can't spend time on why Marshall made his decision, but know that due to his strong Federalist views, his decision has been a thorn in the side to all Americans who believe and support the U.S. Constitution. The *necessary and proper* clause in the Constitution has been used numerous times since to pass political agendas not supported by what many feel is the original intent of our Constitution. This is a subject matter that falls beyond the focus of this book. Just know that the bankers won in 1819 and for the next 15 years stayed in power, making money off the labor of hard-working Americans (sound familiar?). This question of the constitutionality of a central bank became a political controversy throughout the early 1820's.

Thomas Jefferson died in 1826 holding to his belief that any U.S. central bank is unconstitutional, unjust and a detriment to all Americans. I wonder how he felt on his death bed about not succeeding in abolishing the concept of a "central bank" from the political landscape.

A gentleman famous for his leadership during the Battle of New Orleans came on the scene as a follower of Jefferson's views on central banking. General Andrew Jackson, soon to be President Jackson, took up Jefferson's battle. Old Hickory gave the bankers the same fight he gave the "bloody" British in the Battle of New Orleans in 1814. He won again, routing this time the bankers' grip on the money supply of the United States.

Thanks to Jackson's efforts, supported by Jefferson's legacy, the bankers lost their renewal efforts in 1835 to extend another 20 year charter of the 2nd Bank of the United States. Let's take a look at the Andy Jackson era. The cave only gets darker and darker . . .

2ND BANK OF THE UNITED STATES 1815-1835
PHILADELPHIA, PENNSYLVANIA

Bullets Points to Remember

- paper money first appeared in the Colonies in 1690 in Massachusetts

- the Colonies experienced a period of prosperity and good-will in their economy with their "Colonial Scrip," helped by Spain's silver and gold coins until 1750

- England's Currency Law of 1764 forbade the Colonies from creating their own money, which lead to chaos and economic depression; the colonists now "bought" their money from Rothschild Bank of England

- while there are many reasons for the Revolutionary War, Founding Father, Benjamin Franklin felt that the main cause of the War for Independence did not rest with high taxes, but the Bank of England enforcing their will and greed through England's Currency Laws. The colonists revolted against taking away the right to create their own money and the crippling requirement to pay private bankers

- the Continental Congress created a type of Colonial Scrip called the "Continental" to help finance the war with England. Through excessive printing by Congress and counterfeiting by the British, the Continental inflated itself out of existence and gave way to the saying, *"Not Worth a Continental"*

- the first quasi-central bank for the United States was established in 1781 under the direction of Robert Morris. Overrun by corruption and inflating money, The Bank of North America only lasted until 1784. Alexander

Hamilton cut his teeth during this time to emerge as a lead proponent for the 2nd U.S. central bank

- after much debate on both sides of the aisle, the 1st Bank of the United States, under the leadership of then Secretary of the Treasury, Alexander Hamilton, received its charter in 1791. The debate centered around the constitutionality of a central bank, with Jeffersonians on one side and Hamiltonians on the other. This hotly contested debate stayed in the forefront for many years and helped to establish the two distinct political parties that we see today

- in 1811, the charter for the 1st Bank of the U.S. failed muster by one vote and went into oblivion. Strangely, war broke out with Great Britain in 1812. Many historians feel that Nathan Rothschild, head of the Bank of England and main stockholder of the 1st Bank of the U.S., worked behind the scenes and instigated the war with the United States for political and monetary reasons. Throughout history when war breaks out, you can rest assured a banker finances it. Bankers make tons of money financing wars between nations

- the Second Bank of the United States received its charter in 1815 to help eliminate the debt caused by the War of 1812. The new central bank benefited from 20 years of pillaging the people's money, until Andrew Jackson, with the help of Jefferson's legacy put an end to the multi-snaked head of the bank

<u>Key Questions to Ponder</u>

1. What really caused the Revolutionary War?

2. What does "not worth a Continental mean?

3. Why did the Bank of North America fail?

4. Who led the charge for the First Bank of the United States?

5. The Second Bank of the United States received a charter for what reason?

6. What Supreme Court case shot down the unconstitutionality of a central bank?

7. Who stopped the Second Bank of the United States from being re-chartered?

8. What Bank has always had an interest in the affairs of American banking?

"When a government is dependent for money upon bankers, they and not the leaders of that government control the situation, since the hand that gives is above the hand that takes. Money has no motherland; financiers are without patriotism and without decency; their sole object is gain."

-Napoleon Bonaparte, 1807

Author Note: I'm sure the above quote targeted Nathan Rothschild's banking family. During the Napoleonic Wars, the Rothschild dynasty financed both France and Britain. Did they care about the untold suffering and misery caused by these wars? No! They only cared about their bottom line and how much money they could ransack and profit from the people. Especially in recent times, when war clouds appear, bankers are just waiting in the wings with their money schemes to promote, plunder and profit!

V. Jack's Slaying, Abe's Greenbacks & Garfield's Assassination

Andrew Jackson's Bank Battle with Biddle

Remember Jesus' wrath in the Temple? Welcome to another *Den of Thieves*! This is what President Andrew Jackson called the officials of the 2nd Bank of the United States in his monumental battle with the banking industry. President Jackson and the Bank's head man, Nicholas Biddle, went down as the most acrimonious political relationship in U.S. history.

The friction between Jackson and Biddle started in 1829, upon Jackson's ascent to the Presidency. President Jackson understood the banker's deceitful mechanisms that plundered the people's wealth and dedicated his political career and energy to ending the influence of Biddle and his hoard of private bankers.

In some ways, I feel Jackson's actions and beliefs bore similarity to Jesus throwing out the Temple money changers. He saw firsthand the corruption fostered on the American people by the bankers. He allied himself to Jefferson's principles of the unconstitutionality of a central bank. He observed how the Bank caused the first bust in 1819 by tightening the money supply and in turn confiscating the people's money.

He understood the problems and conquered them, but at a terrible price. He was nearly assassinated for his beliefs, but prevailed in his convictions. Thanks to Jackson and his support of the common man, the Second Bank of the United States lost its bid for re-charter in 1835.

GENERAL JACKSON SLAYING THE MANY HEADED MONSTER

'If the American people only understood the rank injustice of our money and banking system, there would be a revolution before morning . . . Hydra-headed monsters eating the flesh of the common man."

The Second Bank of the United States lost its bid for re-charter in 1835.

-Andrew Jackson, 7th US President, 1835

The above quote from Jackson is interesting, because nothing has changed since then. *"A revolution before morning . . ."* WOW! I believe if most Americans truly understood the evil inner workings of the Federal Reserve and what it has done to destroy the sovereignty of this great nation, there would be a revolution of epic proportions. We should take heed and follow Jackson's words. Like Old Hickory, I feel Americans need to rise up and defeat the multi-headed monster before it completely devours us. Sadly, time is running out.

From 1835 to the late 1850's, banking in the United States went through several revisions, none successful in meeting the needs of the people. A constant, continuing fleecing of the people's money up until the Civil War prevailed and it got worse!

History books disregard the true nature of what caused the Civil War between the States. Although, Lincoln abhorred slavery, history shows that many of his speeches didn't support equal rights between the white race and the black race. Understand the poor economic conditions in the late 1850's. The South wanted to export their cotton to Europe in exchange for cheaper European goods. The North excised tariffs on goods from Europe in order to charge higher prices in the South. These factors, not slavery, led to the hostilities. Remember, bankers love conflict and will play both sides against each other for profit. It happened with the Rothschild's in the early 1800's and it happened again before the Civil War. On a personal note, I

> History books disregard the true nature of what caused the Civil War.

believe the institution of slavery added fuel to the fire, and was used by Lincoln in his *Emancipation Proclamation* as a rallying cry and morale builder when the Union needed to win the war.

France, in alliance with Mexico sided with the Confederacy. England massed troops along the Canadian border waiting as an opportunist, ready to pounce at any sign of weakness in Lincoln's Union. You can bet the central bankers in the United States, England and France were right in the thick of things, licking their chops as the war broke out between the North and the South.

> Lincoln above all else wanted to save the Union, even to the point of going against the U.S. Constitution.

Abe and His Greenbacks

For your perusal, a couple of quotes from Abraham Lincoln's political career:

In his inaugural address March 4, 1861 Lincoln said *"I have no purpose, directly or indirectly, to interfere with the institution of slavery in the States where it exists. I believe I have no lawful right to do so, and I have no inclination to do so."*

Later during the Civil War in August 1862, Lincoln again confirmed his stance on slavery -
"My paramount object in this struggle is to save the Union, and is not either to save or to destroy slavery."

Political speak? You decide what really caused the Civil War. The economy of the country at this time lay ripe for war between the States. The North and South were at odds with each other over money, goods, services and tariffs. The bankers were

LINCOLN'S GREENBACKS

more than happy to perpetuate the conflict between the American people. As previously stated, bankers put their hands in the money pot when war appears on the horizon.

Remember that Lincoln above all else wanted to save the Union, even to the point of going against the U.S. Constitution. The Constitution specifically forbade the government from emitting "bills of credit" or paper money. But, when a nation goes to war and in this case the "to save the Union," it needs money to finance that war. Congress looked for a quick fix for its growing appetite to fund the Civil War, so in 1862 they authorized the Treasury to print $150 million worth of bills of credit. The notes printed in a distinctive green ink became known as *"Greenbacks."* Unconstitutional? Yes, but needed to save the Union.

Lincoln, according to history, showed himself as two-faced concerning his feelings about bankers. Early in his political career, he supported Biddle and the 2nd Bank of the United States, but later went against the banker's debt money by creating the government's own money in the form of

Greenbacks. As you can imagine, the bankers didn't like the government taking over the nation's money supply. The circulating Greenbacks replaced the banker's fiat debt money and caused the bankers to lobby Congress with the support of Treasurer, Salmon Chase, for a different monetary system. The National Bank Act became law in 1863.

Lincoln privately feared the Bank Act. He, like Jackson and Jefferson before him saw the corruption when private bankers controlled the people's money. He wanted to keep order in his administration and do everything he could to save his dear Union and let the Bank Act pass without veto. The Act created a new system of National Banks that separately operated like a central bank, but under the auspices of Washington. The bankers had a sweet operation, dealing government bonds, charging interest on those bonds and then lending out the money made from those bonds and charging interest again. In essence they made money coming and going, just like they do today.

Lincoln's plan to reverse the National Bank Act was evident in the 1864 Republican Party Platform: *"10. Resolved, That the National faith, pledged for the redemption of the public debt, must be kept inviolate, and that for this purpose we recommend economy and rigid responsibility in the public expenditures, and a vigorous and just system of taxation; and that it is the duty of every loyal state to sustain the credit and promote the use of the National currency."* Greenbacks were our nation's first attempt to create a National Currency. Unfortunately, on April 14, 1865 Lincoln was assassinated.

Many historians and books report that John Wilkes Booth assassinated Lincoln. Others feel that he died at the hands of a group called *Knights of the Golden Circle*. Was Booth a member of the KGC? This group had rumored ties with U.S. politicians and British financiers (Rothschilds again?). One fact is known: Lincoln espoused harsh words for bankers and came to understand the evils associated with central bankers.

Was Lincoln murdered by a Southern sympathizer (Booth) or evil political forces in the shadows offstage? You decide! Lincoln's assassination does not stand as the only time a sitting President might have been eliminated by the Money Power.

Garfield's Assassination

James Garfield, who became our 20th President, was known as a gold standard man. He was an expert in finance. In his March, 1881 inaugural address he stated "By the experience of commercial nations in all ages it has been found that gold and silver afford the only safe foundation for a monetary system. ... The finances of the Government shall suffer no detriment, which it may be possible for my Administration to prevent".

President Garfield was assassinated just six months after making the above statement. Did he offend the bankers or was he eliminated by some crazed gunman with a questionable mental status?

Though I'm not a conspiracy theorist, it is suspicious to me that when a prominent government official such as the President of the United States, says something derogatory against bankers (Garfield) or goes against their programs (Jackson & Lincoln), they were murdered or an assassination attempt was made. What is going on here? It happened again in 1963.

I'm surprised that Jefferson lived to a ripe old age. Maybe history didn't record an assassination attempt on his life. Whatever reason, the elite bankers are very powerful people as we shall see.

<u>Bullets Points to Remember</u>

- fighting for the common man, President Jackson took on Nicholas Biddle and defeated the renewal charter of the 2nd Bank of the United States in 1835

- from 1835 to the late 1850's, several different "banking" programs were attempted, but failed due to the constant debasement of the people's money and the bankers enriching their pockets

- Abraham Lincoln in his early political career supported Biddle and his central bankers, but later in his career came out against the deceit and corruption of having to pay private bankers for the privilege of using their money

- above all else, Lincoln desired to save the Union and allowed the U.S. government to produce its own paper money in the form of Greenbacks

- the Civil War was not fought over slavery, but over money and economics between the States; the South sold cotton to Europe and bought their goods cheaper than buying from the North; in turn, the North put heavy tariffs on goods sold to South

- some historians feel Lincoln was assassinated by the Money Power due to his support of the government creating the people's money

- in 1881, President James Garfield was murdered after speaking out against the bankers

<u>Key Questions to Ponder</u>

1. Who was the head of the Second Bank of the United States?

2. What did Jackson call the central bankers in a famous quote?

3. Slavery is the history book's answer to the cause of the Civil War, but what really precipitated the hostilities between the North and South?

4. What are Greenbacks? What did Lincoln have to do to fund the Civil War and how   did the bankers react?

5. Why did Lincoln turn against the bankers later in his political career?

". . . to come to an agreement on the structure and operation of a banking cartel. The goal of the cartel, as is true with all of them, was to maximize profits by minimizing competition between members, to make it difficult for new competitors to enter the field, and to utilize the police power of the government to enforce the cartel agreement."

The purpose of the Jekyll Island meeting . . .
G. Edward Griffin, <u>The Creature from Jekyll Island</u>, 2002, pg. 8

VI. Birth of the Beast and ...
It needs to be FED!!

Jekyll Island

> The middle class has paid a hidden tax called **inflation** ever since the FED's beginning.

THE BIRTH OF THE BEAST!! Sounds ominous and scary. The only scary aspect lies in the appetite this animal owns and how much it consumes. This Beast eats a lot of green paper! Before we go into the culinary delicacies and diet of the Beast, we need to go to the year 1910 and Jekyll Island, Georgia. At this locale, America's modern banking system was born. It wasn't a pretty sight.

Privately owned, Jekyll Island sits off the coast of Georgia and served as a perfect place to hold a secret meeting between international financiers and U.S. politicians. The meeting's purpose centered on hatching something called the Federal Reserve. Understand, the clandestine "get together" contained a perfect liaison between government and finance and similar to the illicit collusion that now exists between the FED, Wall Street bankers and our government. Can you imagine the fallout and chaos if the public knew that these "connected" bankers and politicians were secretly meeting to develop a banking cartel? Like a snake hiding in plain sight, they now do it in the open for all to see!

An important point to remember is they promoted the Federal Reserve to the American people on the premise that it would control *inflation* and *prevent bank failures.* In 1907, the U.S. experienced colossal problems in the banking industry. The monetary scientists at the time named the banking upheaval the *Bank Panic of 1907.* Because of bank failures across the country, the people clamored for regulations and an end to the monopoly the New York banks had over the rest of the country. This situation led to the bankers and politicians getting together to formulate another U.S. central bank under the disguise of mitigating the people's banking concerns. The ruse began on an island off the coast of Georgia under a pretense of calming the calamity and instilling order in the banking industry and financial markets. The resultant Federal Reserve has been a complete failure in its purpose and stated functions (see Other Topics).

The FED has done nothing in almost 100 years to put a lid on inflation or to control bank failures. In fact, our U.S. dollar has lost over 95% of its value since 1913 (see Appendix). Case in point: back in 1972, I purchased a new car off the lot for $2,200.00, including tax, tag and title. Today, in U.S. dollars that same car would cost 7 times what I paid. Many factors are responsible for the increase, but the main cause

> Our U.S. dollar has lost over 95% of its value since 1913.

is that our dollar is not worth what it was back in the early 70's. Another way to say this is that it takes more dollars to purchase the same goods and services as compared to 40 years ago. Debasing our money and uncontrolled inflation has wrecked our dollar. Every time the FED injects their fiat paper money into our financial systems, our dollars lose value. It's no wonder that senior citizens on fixed incomes are upset with earning a measly .5% interest on their $1,000.00 certificate of deposit (CD), while the value of the dollar goes into a tailspin.

Also, Americans could purchase $1 worth of goods with $1 silver dollar before 1913. Now that $1 is worth less than a nickel in goods. Tell me if that isn't progress! And here's the kicker: *The middle class has paid a hidden tax called inflation* ever since the FED's beginning. On this fact alone, the Federal Reserve should be abolished for outright lying to the American people. In 2008, instead of controlling the financial operations of several Wall Street investment banks and mortgage institutions, the FED let them run wild with their easy money and the banker's fancy derivative games. We all know the results of this lack of oversight and malfeasance. The major players haven't faced judgment or scrutiny and still operate in an environment that favors them.

Republican Senator Nelson Aldrich stood as the lead politician at this confidential Jekyll Island meeting, followed by representatives from the Rothschild's (there's that name again!) and Rockefeller's. The House of Rothschild exemplified international banking financiers and the Rockefeller's were connected with energy and big oil. These men represented the *Who's Who* of the banking and business world in combination with the movers and shakers in the U.S. government. They discussed and promoted another central bank for the United States (the 4th). The name "Federal Reserve" was chosen specifically to fool the American people to think that it had something to do with the Federal government. The name also allowed them to trick the people into believing the Federal Reserve possessed lots of "reserves" in its vaults. The Federal Reserve is NOT federal and owns NO reserves!! Unfortunately, this meeting makes up only the beginning of the ruse. For almost 100 years, the American people have allowed the FED to exist.

December 23, 1913, the Federal Reserve Act

On the above date, the people's constitutional right to their money and property went out the window. When most politicians in Washington reveled on holiday recess (sound familiar), the Federal Reserve Act was passed in Congress under the disguise of *"Progressivism."* President Woodrow Wilson, catering to the people who put him in office, signed the Federal Reserve Act into law. The central bankers and monetary scientists took control and haven't let go! It's interesting to note, the very next year the United States went to war in Europe. Did the bankers know something that Wilson didn't know? Paul Warburg, considered the Father of the Federal Reserve, and his brother Max had ties to Germany.

"...the fact that his brother was head of the German Secret Service, while his family banking house, M.M. Warburg Company of Hamburg and Amsterdam, was playing its role of chief financial agent for the Kaiser. We had been at war for

53

more than a year before Paul Warburg thought he should resign."

-A Study of the Federal Reserve and its Secrets,
Mullins, Eustace, 2010, p. 52

Did the Warburg brothers acquire a leg up in influencing the U.S. entry into WWI? You can bet they came prepared to sell their cheap, interest-laden money to finance the war. One took care of the United States, while the other helped Germany. What a deal! In my opinion, and just conjecture, maybe the Federal Reserve came into existence knowing that the U.S. would eventually have to go to war with Germany. After all, someone needed to provide funds at interest for manpower, equipment and food to wage war. While the bankers on both sides of the ocean were raking in the cash, people suffered horrible deaths in the trenches of Europe in the "War to end all Wars."

SIGNING THE FEDERAL RESERVE ACT

Incidentally, Wilson, after he left political office, stated that signing the Federal Reserve Act into law was the worse piece of legislation he ever supported while in office. At least he admitted his mistake. Without knowing, Wilson and his band of "Progressives" started the ball rolling for the systematic transfer of the people's money into the pockets of private bankers. It's called stealing and it's been going on since 1913.

> The FED controls our money either by *TIGHTENING* the supply or by *EXPANDING* the supply.

The First Bust, 1920-21 . . . Sorry Farmers!

Before we start discussing the "vile acts of evil" the Federal Reserve perpetrates on the American people, understand the FED controls our money either by *TIGHTENING* the supply or by *EXPANDING* the supply. You must grasp this important concept in order to understand the ramifications of what the FED does.

Many economic theories abound as to what causes what. I will leave the theories, explanations and working of economics to the experts and scholars. The Keynes, Mises, Pigoos and Kindlebergers *et al* have the knowledge and intellect to explain the intricacies of economy as to why it grows, shrinks, recesses, depresses and inflates. Technical books are abundant with economic theory and involved equations that have complicated results and are difficult to understand – ideas and compilations that go far beyond the purpose of this book. For example, some economists feel the Farming Depression of 1920 came about due to high commodity prices from World War I. I'm sure the economists at the time sat at tables, twirled their handlebar moustaches and through their theories and numbers looked at the commodity prices and tried to explain why farming went into a depression. A pure academic adventure that fluffed the feathers of the economists, but did nothing to explain the real reason for the collapse of the farming economy.

Concerning the study of money, John Kenneth Galbraith says it best on page 5 from his book, <u>Money: Whence it Came, Where it Went</u>, 1975, *"The study of money, above all other fields in economics, is one in which complexity is used to disguise truth or to evade truth, not to reveal it."*

From a layman/farmer point of view the main cause of the depression was the Federal Reserve taking money from the farmers, mainly, the farmers living in the Midwest and West. They tightened the money supply and called in the loans. Farmers before the FED action enjoyed the good life. They bought land and paid off their mortgages. The FED decided to call in the money. Then the Federal Reserve member banks foreclosed and confiscated the farmer's wealth and property.

The above scam began at the Federal Reserve's inception and continues today. Remember, that every Boom and Bust in the economy owes its cause to the FED's monetary policy. Either they pour cheap debt money into the economy or pull back the reins and say. *"Ho, horsey. Let's break the backs of the people. Then let's pick up the pieces and stuff our pockets with money and assets from the inevitable monetary collapse."* Banks foreclosing on home/farm mortgages allows them to confiscate hard assets. Is that fair?

In 2008, this very thing happened and continues to occur. It doesn't matter whether the bankers are ramping up the economy or breaking it down, they make money both ways.

Louis McFadden, Chairman of the House Banking Committee, 1920-1931, said about the Federal Reserve Banks, *"A world banking system was being set up here . . . A super-state controlled by international bankers and international industrialists acting together to enslave the world for their own pleasure. The FED has usurped the government."*

At least one politician understood the dirty deeds of the FED. Senator McFadden, on several occasions, took on the FED, lambasting them for their corrupt ways. He was eventually murdered after being shot twice and poisoned twice. The second poisoning incident silenced him. Remember folks, we deal with very powerful and connected people.

The Great Depression - 1929

> Every Boom and Bust in the economy owes its cause to the FED's monetary policy.

I recall my father telling me about the big bank and stock market failure of '29 and the resultant economic depression. He said his mother would make a huge bowl of stock chicken soup with a few veggies thrown in and this entailed what he and his siblings would eat for a week. Times were tough, not unlike today. The "soup kitchen" came into vogue in 1929. Basically, one day the American people lived the good life, the next, they woke up to a day of reckoning.

The Great Depression is a prime example of the Federal Reserve's and banking industry's treachery. When the people "run" a bank, good luck if you ever get your money back. When people lose confidence, the stock

JOBLESS MEN
KEEP GOING
WE CAN'T TAKE CARE OF OUR OWN

market seeks a bottom. This scenario happened on *Black Tuesday*, October 29th, 1929 when the financial markets and banks hit the skids, leading to a decade of economic turmoil.

The banks and the stock market took a big hit leaving the American people empty handed and desolate. Remember the Roaring Twenties? Remember flappers, bath tub gin and a dance called the Charleston? If you don't know about the good life in the 1920's, then ask your parents or grandparents, or better yet, google it. What brought about the fun times?

If you guessed an expansion of money and credit by the Federal Reserve, then go to the front of the line. What do you think caused the Great Depression? Answer: the FED on August 9, 1929 stuck a pin in the balloon, burst the bubble and increased the bank-loan rate. Then, they began to sell securities in the open market. The economy started to break apart, hitting close to dead-bottom on that fateful day in October.

> The outbreak of WW II is what finally brought an end to the Great Depression.

By deliberately manipulating the money supply to the downside, they essentially reduced the supply, or "tightened" it, causing an economic panic that lasted for several years. To make matters worse, the federal government instituted a multitude of programs and regulations to exacerbate the problem.

FDR and his "New Deal" pumped more money into the economy. All this fresh money and government programs were enacted to restart the country on a track to recovery. The government intervening, controlling and messing with prices all combined to prevent the recovery from ever leaving the starting gate. Not until this country got on a war footing through the outbreak of World War II did the Great Depression find its way to the trash pile. Sad, but true, we can thank the war for bringing back the economy.

Contrary to popular opinion, no evidence exist that the powers-that-be caused the Crash for the purpose of profit taking. The monetary scientist possessed the means to avert the catastrophe, but other agendas took precedent. The Money Changers didn't know or want to know the complete picture. Once they understood the coming calamity, they instead saved their own skins at the expense of the people they were sworn to protect. Did they make money? No, but they didn't lose any either.

According to G. Edward Griffin, on page 497 from his book, The Creature from Jekyll Island, "*John D. Rockefeller, J.P. Morgan, Joseph P. Kennedy, Bernard Baruch, Henry Morganthau, Douglas Dillon—the biographies of all the Wall Street giants at that time boast that these men were "wise" enough to get out of the stock market just before the Crash. And it is true. Virtually all of the inner club was rescued.*"

Recently, ghosts of the past have re-visited us. Ask tax-evader, now Secretary of the Treasury, Tim Geithner, or former Secretary of the Treasury and also former Goldman-Sachs Chairman, Henry Paulson, if they lost money in the big 2008 Bust? I know I did. These elite bankers stick together like peas in a pod and here's proof.

How can a tax-evader get appointed to Secretary of the Treasury? Geithner was the head of the powerful New York Federal Reserve bank. Do you think they take care of each other? Can it get it worse? You bet your bottom fake dollar it can!! Ask Franklin Delano Roosevelt.

Bail Out of the FED and the People's Confiscation of Gold, 1933

Franklin Delano Roosevelt's (FDR) gold confiscation of 1933 served as a bailout of the Federal Reserve. This stands as one of many examples where the U.S. government sided with the private bankers at the expense of the American people.

> Franklin D. Roosevelt's gold confiscation of 1933 served as a bailout of the Federal Reserve.

President Roosevelt's Executive Order 6102 on April 5, 1933, outlawed the private ownership of gold in the United States. Arguably, unconstitutional and evoking some archaic Emergency Order from WW I, FDR basically stole the people's money. Some historians feel that he called in the gold to get the economy moving again and to stop people from "hoarding" the yellow precious metal. Recall, that the country wallowed in a depression and stashing precious metals under your bed increased one's sense of security in difficult economic times. Roosevelt took the gold to prop up the gold reserves of the privately-owned FED.

Paper money has always been suspect in the United States. Common sense tells you that Americans would always choose a $20 gold coin over a $20

1882 GOLD CERTIFICATE

piece of paper. To increase the validity of paper money and the confidence of the people, the U.S. Treasury insured gold and silver certificates and stated on the paper they could be redeemed at face value in gold and silver coin.

The people of the United States assumed that the Treasury held enough gold and silver to back the certificates. An example of this is a $100 gold certificate would be exchanged for five $20 gold coins. Without the specific redeemable notations on these certificates, the populace would be less likely to accept them in commerce.

When the Federal Reserve came into existence in 1913, they issued their own Federal Reserve Notes (FRN's) the next year. These FRN's originally received backing by precious metals and stated on the note they could be traded in for gold or silver. As time passed, more and more paper FRN's made it into circulation. The quantity of dollars increased dramatically. This led to the Roaring Twenties and then to the "Crash of 29" as previously discussed. Both instances trace their cause to the Federal Reserve either increasing or decreasing the money supply.

Banks happily "lent" out easy paper dollars increasing the FRN's in circulation. Remember, for every dollar that the FED and banks lend, they charge interest. This money (sic) is owed back to the FED or whoever purchased the government bond or

> Every dollar in circulation created by the Federal Reserve from 1914 through 2012 is debt money.

treasury instrument. China owns most of the U.S. debt. If they call our hand or stop purchasing our debt money i.e. t-bills, government bonds, etc our economy would experience a total meltdown. Can you imagine the chaos if that would happen? It would be 1929 all over again, but much worse.

Every dollar in circulation created by the Federal Reserve from 1914 through 2012 is debt money. Before the Federal Reserve, any American could go to a bank, put down his $20 gold certificate and get one $20 gold coin in return. When the FED came on the scene, the "Gold Standard" went out the window.

We will return to this "debt money machine" in later chapters and how the Gold Standard keeps bankers honest. Just know for now that when we use FRN's it comes from the debt of others!

The credit contraction led to the Stock Market Crash and the Great Depression. Everyone suddenly became reluctant to borrow. Banks were afraid to lend and the movement of money in circulation came to a halt. Unknown to the American public, the constant flow of gold certificate-backed FRN's into the economy without a corresponding amount of species (gold) to cover the FRN's led to FDR in 1933 confiscating the people's gold and giving it to the Federal Reserve.

Not only did he give this money away, but the people lost even more when he raised the gold price from twenty to thirty-five dollars per ounce. These actions

> Roosevelt sold out the American people to international bankers and the Federal Reserve.

covered the FED's losses and placated the European central banks which held substantial quantities of U.S. gold notes. This action by FDR is just another example of government and bankers getting together to cause economic turmoil and misery for the American people.

What happened in a nutshell? Roosevelt sold out the American people to international bankers and the Federal Reserve. The privately-owned FED didn't have the gold to cover what they owed, so "We the People" bailed them out. The entire U.S. monetary system changed and the debt-laden, paper-thin, worthless FRN's became the medium of exchange, backed only by legal tender laws and the good faith of the United States. Some historians and economists feel the United States lost its sovereignty in 1933 and have been beholden to the international bankers ever since.

FRANKLIN D. ROOSEVELT

Speaking about gold, many people and conspiracy theorists feel that the "people's" gold no longer resides at Fort Knox, Kentucky. If there's any gold, it's of questionable quality.

Many congressmen, especially Representative Ron Paul from Texas, tried for years to audit the gold at Fort Knox to no avail. The U.S. Treasury Department, headed by Tim Geithner, the former head of the FED's New York division, stonewalls anyone who wants to know about the gold at Fort Knox. Many feel that most of the gold was shipped to the Bank of England in the late 1960's. Has the government been fooling the American people?

As recently as June, 2011, Ron Paul asked for a full audit of the gold at Fort Knox. Paul, who wants to covert the U.S. monetary system to one based on the Gold Standard, says the federal government owes it to the taxpayers to make sure U.S. owned gold is safe. He stated, *"This is one of the legitimate functions of government to check our ownership and be fiscally responsible and find out just what we own and whether it's really there."*

He also added that the FED of New York owns 5% of the U.S. gold reserves and possesses the ability to secretly sell or swap gold with other countries without any one knowing. The people should demand that a third party, not the "fox in the henhouse"

> Central bankers throughout history have been taking money from the people through their illicit money schemes and games.

Geithner's Treasury audit the gold reserves at Knox and at the N.Y. FED. Only then will the people know the truth.

Central bankers throughout history have been taking money from the people through their illicit money schemes and games. Is there a government cover-up? Is our gold missing from Fort Knox? Do your own investigation for the truth.

Bretton Woods, IMF & World Bank - 1944

After the fleecing by FDR of the people's gold in 1933, the world fell head first into a World War II. The central bankers of the world loved the turmoil and quickly and without hesitation helped to ignite the war machines of Germany, Russia, Japan and the United States. All the while they fanned the fires with their easy credit and debt money. Many sources report that several U.S. financiers supported Hitler's rise to power in the 1930's. As in the Napoleonic Wars of the early 1800's, bankers on both sides provided the means to pay for the human toil, bullets, bombs and beans, which resulted in millions of deaths, misery and destruction.

> Many sources report that several U.S. financiers supported Hitler's rise to power in the 1930's.

Towards the end of hostility in 1944, the central bankers decided they needed something in place to assist with the negotiations and reparations of the soon-to-be defeated Tri-Axis of Germany, Italy and Japan. In other words, they wanted to consolidate their power. The central bankers met in little Bretton Woods, New Hampshire and created the framework for the International Monetary Fund (IMF) and the World Bank.

Under the guise of providing needed funding to help the war-torn countries get back on their feet and get their economies going again, the bankers created on a world scale a model based on our own Federal Reserve.

Just like our FED, they could print money out of nothing and charge interest on it. This time they extended their evil grip on nations around the world, specifically third world countries. The World

> Much of the poverty in third world countries stems from excessive debt-money owed to the bankers who run the World Bank.

Bank provided their fiat money to developing countries in the form of loans and credit. When a country couldn't pay the debt down, they started to confiscate the country's property and assets. What's currently happening (2012) in Europe, and Greece in particular is a result of the IMF and World Bank monetary policies. These organizations have what I call a "pumping" syndrome – infusing tons of fake money into the European economy. The European international central bankers are debasing the Euro and creating false prosperity and inflation. I believe this scenario is coming to our shores sooner then we think.

Much of the poverty in third world countries stem from excessive debt-money owed to the bankers who run the World Bank. This "program of assistance" looks similar to our banks giving out loans and when things turn bad and the people can't pay, the *banksters* (a needed lexicon) foreclose, taking the property with them.

What a swindle, and it's now happening on an international stage. If a country can't pay its debt to the IMF, they become insolvent and eventually lose their sovereignty. Then they become servants to the private international bankers.

The bankers, through the Bretton Woods Agreements, created a private banking cartel of the world's privately owned central banks. Then they assumed the power to dictate policies to banks of all nations. This whole scenario is very similar to when the Bank of England, through the English Parliament, enacted Currency Laws forbidding the colonists from printing their own money in 1764.

The developing nations of the world have to go to a middle man just like the colonists, and "buy" their money through the IMF and World Bank. Every time I think about what these crooked central bankers have done to humanity throughout history, the thoughts put me in a depressing funk.

The Council of Foreign Relations (CFR) played a huge role in the formulation of the IMF and World Bank. What is the CFR: according to Mike Kirchubel, from his book, <u>Vile Acts of Evil</u>, the CFR it is a highly influential organization of businessmen and experts set up by the Morgan's (Rothschild's) after WW I to promote an internationalist foreign political and economic policy. **Influential connected people scratching the backs of other influential connected people**. That's what a banking cartel is all about!

Are YOU mad yet?

Time for a Breather . . .?

I don't know about you, but I'm hot under the collar. Maybe we need to take a break. In the interim, based on what you have read so far, your previous experiences and knowledge, can you think of anything the Federal Reserve has done to benefit the sovereignty of the United States? This question is not a joke. I want to hear the other side of the story. If you know of anything that the FED has done to give us a stable monetary system now is the time to get published. If so, please make notes and fill-in the above space and send your comments to: jimac49@yahoo.com. When I do a 2nd printing of this book, I want to include your comments under the heading, *The Fabulous FED!*

Another Black Spot?

> JFK wanted to enact legislation that went against the status quo, namely, the military and the central bankers.

Before we head to the beginning of the 20th century, many people feel that John F. Kennedy's assassination was carried out by forces who wanted him out of the presidency and not by a disgruntled, lone gunman. Whether it was the CIA, FBI, or Cuba operatives or some other unknown entity, I'm convinced that Lee Harvey Oswald didn't act alone in Deely Plaza that fateful day in November, 1963. If you research the events leading up to November 22, 1963, you will find out that Kennedy signed into law *Executive Order 11110* on June 4th, 1963. In essence, the order had the effect of allowing the U.S. Treasury to issue silver backed dollars against any silver in the U.S. Treasury. In other words, silver backed dollars could be issued and not tied to the Federal Reserve. And get this: *WITH NO INTEREST OR DEBT ATTACHED.* Kennedy, basically, signed into law a way for the U.S. government to *CREATE* its own money independent of the FED. By signing this order, Kennedy, eliminated the middle-man and stopped the insanity of paying interest on Federal Reserve Notes. Some people feel that Executive Order 11110 is still in effect and hasn't been repealed.

According to Don Stott in an article that appeared May 3, 2007 concerning Executive Order 11110, he states, *"Kennedy knew what was going on at the FED, Vietnam, Cuba, and the CIA.*

> We need politicians with honest insight and virtue, like our Founding Fathers.

He attempted to stop it. His Executive Order 11110 would have been the beginning of the end for the FED, and we might still be a solvent nation without the last 44 years of interest from un-backed currency printing accumulating debt. The funny thing is that Executive Order 11110 has not been reversed, voted out, nor cancelled."

-Colorado Gold

JFK wanted to enact legislation that went against the status quo, namely, the military and the central bankers. The military-industrial complex, prepping for the Vietnam War, needed the bankers. Central bankers love war. JFK saw through both of them. First, he wanted to bring home the few troops (advisors) which had already been shipped to Vietnam. Second, he saw the illicit manipulation of the nation's money supply by the FED (JFK probably read Thomas Jefferson's rants against a central bank) and wanted the United States to start producing its own money and end the Federal Reserve once and for all. Third, he saw the CIA (Central Intelligence Agency) as a redundant organization that didn't serve the best interests of the American people.

Many feel Kennedy was murdered by the CIA. Some feel he was assassinated by the Money Powers for his stance on the FED's debt-laden monetary policies and wanting to return honest money to America. Whatever happened, JFK stood up against the powerful few and was silenced. Do your own research on this one. If Kennedy could have instituted an honest money system, and eliminated the debt producing policies of the FED, we would not be looking at trillions in debt today!

John Kennedy had his demons, but we need more politicians like him to get this country back on track. We need politicians with honest insight and virtue, like our Founding Fathers. To them, serving their country was an honor and privilege, not a position to distort, use or take for granted. The elite wanted to pigeon-hole JFK, but he fought for the American people instead of caving into special interests. We need more politicians, who are willing to fight for the common man and stop the powerful few from taking over this great country and the world!

JOHN F. KENNEDY, 11-22-63

Author's Note: *Term Limits should be made into law to prevent politicians from growing roots and running the roost in Congress. These people get into a position of power and forget their scruples, which lead to unholy alliances and collusion with the Money Power.*

<u>Bullet Points to Remember</u>

- world financiers and politician met on Jekyll Island, GA in 1910 to plan the 4th central bank of the United States

- the Federal Reserve came into being on December 23, 1913

- the Federal Reserve was created to control inflation and have done nothing to control this hidden tax on the middle class; in fact, the U.S. dollar has lost over 95% of its value through inflation since the FED's beginning in 1913

- the first bust came in 1920-21, when the money supply was tightened and the farmers suffered a deep depression

- the Roaring 20's was caused by an expansion of Federal Reserve Notes

- the Crash of 1929, which led to the Great Depression, was caused by the FED's monetary policy of contracting the money supply

- the United States lost its sovereignty when President Roosevelt confiscated the people's gold in 1933

- The Bretton Woods Agreement in 1944 established the International Monetary Fund and the World Bank, insuring and assuring the continued control of central bankers around the world

- President John F. Kennedy, through Executive Order 11110, wanted the U.S. government to start producing its own money backed by silver in May, 1963

- Executive Order 11110, signed by JFK is still on the books and has not been repealed

<u>Key Questions to Ponder</u>

1. What secret meeting took place on Jekyll Island, Georgia in 1910?

2. Why was the Federal Reserve signed into law?

3. What caused the Depression of 1920-21?

4. The Stock Market Crash of 1929 led to the Depression; what factors caused these economic events to happen?

5. Why did FDR confiscate the people's gold?

6. The Bretton Agreement of 1944 was a disguise for what?

7. Through Executive Order 11110, JFK wanted to do what?

"The banks - it's hard to believe in a time when we're facing a banking crisis that many of the banks created are still the most powerful lobby on Capitol Hill. And they frankly own the place"

-U.S. Senator Dick Durbin, April 27, 2009
Interview with WJJG Radio

> Throughout U.S. history, the central bankers have fleeced the American people again, and again, and again.

VII. Current Money Scheme - 2008 Bust

The current money scheme: <u>NOTHING HAS CHANGED</u> Same old, same old.

Throughout U.S. history, the central bankers have fleeced the American people again, and again, and again. The recent economic downturn proves no different. The Bush Bank Bail-Out of 2008 became the biggest money scam ever fostered on the American people. This fiasco echoed the same thing that Teddy Roosevelt did in 1907. Teddy paid off his banker friend and Rothschild agent J.P. Morgan, as he changed his presidential hat for private life.

We made it to 2012 and bank foreclosures are still running rampant. The bail-out did absolutely nothing to correct the housing foreclosure problems. Crisis like these happened before when taxpayers paid for the "moral hazard" associated with the bank's laize-faire attitude *"that if we get into trouble with our poor lending practices, the American taxpayer will pick-up the tab."*

> Bush's 2008 Bail-Out Bill usurped the U.S. Constitution and forbade any Judicial Review.

This country's financial woes mimic a situation akin to spending your wad at the blackjack table knowing your wife will bail you out, put you to bed and then make breakfast in the morning for you. You, no doubt, have an understanding wife. Like the ocean liner Titanic, banks have this invincible attitude. When they take risky chances and fail, banks should sink like the Titanic. Instead of the loss of lives, as in the tragic sinking of the Titanic, there's a loss of life's savings. Ask any retiree who has worked long and hard, only to have the bankers steal money and equity in his house through risky, illicit investments. The gambler who doesn't know when to stop has a disease and just like our financial institutions, both need to be put on the wagon.

Bush's 2008 Bail-Out Bill usurped the U.S. Constitution and forbade any Judicial Review. The bill allowed the banks to spend the money in any way they wanted. In the end, the bill served as a gift to Bush's big political supporters and the largest transfer of taxpayer money to the bankers in history. The people were lied to and told that the money would be used to lend to businesses and consumers. . . to help with the economy . . . to help these "poor" bankers . . . to prevent something worse from happening. I often wonder where our economy would be today if that $800 billion bank bail-out went instead to the American people.

Mike Kirchubel, in his book, Vile Acts of Evil, summarizes on page 402, an article by New York Times economic columnist, Joe Nocera, commenting on the bank bail-out, *"Its real aim was to bankroll a rapid consolidation of the American banking system by subsidizing a wave of takeovers of smaller financial firms by the most powerful banks."*

We all know what should have happened. The American people should not have been liable for these privately-run corporations.

When a hard-working American, who falls on tough economic times can't pay his bills, do we see these banking and credit corporations bailing him out? No, they immediately call the bill collector. They should have failed, but the powers-that-be recognized an opportunity and took advantage of us poor slobs again. We don't share in their corporate profits, so why should we pay for their business mistakes?

With regard to the 2008 Bush Bust, just know it was another prime example of the unlawful collusion between big business and crooked politicians. Also, know that if the Federal Reserve didn't provide a pipeline flowing with easy money and credit to the investment Wall Street Banks, they wouldn't have the money to risk and then make us pay.

All of those derivative-type securities came into existence out of free money from the FED. Those easy mortgages given to questionable lenders happened because the banks backstroked in unrestricted money give-away. The banks and mortgage companies were swimming in a cesspool of greed and corruption.

Because of the unconstrained money and illicit lending practices, I lost over $50,000 on the house I sold in 2011. I needed to bring money to the table to close the deal after paying dutifully on my $1,200.00/month mortgage. Including the $50,000 loss, I paid close to $200,000 to my bank to live in my house for 10 years. I walked away with nothing, while these rich bankers on Wall Street padded their wallets with extra money and bonuses. The banks stole money from me and you. If we don't do something about their greed and graft, they will continue to do it again and again!

Here's our friend, President Andrew Jackson, *"Gentlemen! I too have been a close observer of the doings of the Bank of the United States. I have had men watching you for a long time, and am convinced that you have used the funds of the bank to speculate in the breadstuffs of the country. When you won, you divided the profits amongst you, and when you lost, you charged it to the bank."*

The major Wall Street Banks took the American people to the bank for a tune of 2 trillion dollars in 2008. Where did all of that money go? First of all, most of it exists as digits, some was paid back, but most of it went into the coffers of the banks and the pockets of the bank executives. The last I looked banks still pay their executive staffs huge bonuses as the country remains in a recession.

> The major Wall Street Banks took the American people to the bank for a tune of two trillion dollars in 2008.

Also, do any of you find it unbelievable that Wall Street breaks new highs daily? Since 2008, Wall Street has risen in value across the board. It seems the brokers on Wall Street and the investment bankers are doing well, while the people suffer. If your 401K is looking better, investors beware! It's just a matter of time before the investment banks bust the market and reap the profits from the turmoil. Why can't the American people see the absurdity in what's happening in our banking industry? They jack up the stock market prices and break it down . . . again, and again and again. The middle class suffers every time.

The FED takes care of their own and that's the prime reason why the rich get richer and the poor get poorer. Sorry to use this cliché, but it rings so true to what is happening in the United States today.

If the above doesn't get you upset, then you are a half-dead and should try out for a part in the next Zombie movie.

Here are two quotes from two very different eras and people:

"While free markets tend to democratize a society, unfettered capitalism leads invariably to corporate control of government."

-Robert Kennedy, Jr.
Rolling Stones Magazine Article "Crimes Against Nature"
December 11, 2003

"Fascism should more properly be called Corporatism, since it is the merger of state and corporate power."

-Attributed to Benito Mussolini
"Vile Acts of Evil, page 411, Michael Kirchubel
(Unable to confirm authenticity)

You decide. After the Crony Capitalism of the Big Bank Bailout of 2008, do we live in a Free Market or Corporatism?

Mussolini would be proud of how Crony Capitalism has taken over the Free Market!

> The FED takes care of their own and that's the prime reason why the rich get richer and the poor get poorer.

Bullet Points to Remember

- the current money scheme is the same as 100 years ago when the FED came into existence

- the Bush-Bailouts of Banks in 2008 are the most expensive fleecing of the American taxpayer in history

- Crony Capitalism was in full swing in 2008; the American taxpayer, as in previous years, paid for the "moral hazard" of bankers taking risks without ramifications

- people lost money in the housing mortgage failure and in their retirement funds, while bankers profited from the free money the government "gave" to the financial institutions

Key Questions to Ponder

1. What caused the Bust in 2008?

2. Why did Bush bail-out the bankers?

3. Why is Wall Street breaking highs, while the economy burns?

4. What should have happened when the banks failed?

5. What is Crony Capitalism?

"There is nothing wrong with your television set. Do not attempt to adjust the picture. We are controlling transmission . . . For the next hour, sit quietly and we will control all that you see and hear."

-Outer Limits, ABC TV series 1963-65

VIII. The Big Picture & Beyond

I remember the *Outer Limits*. The television screen would first go blank and then go into some crazy gyration and a deep, commanding voice would come on and say the above. Certainly, a great piece of marketing that propelled the

> The Patriot Act should have been called the Big Brother Act.

television industry at the time. The powers-that-be stole a clue from the 60's sci-fi program and are working the concept to their advantage by keeping us docile and in the dark.

It's funny that George Orwell's book, *1984,* slaps us right in our face. I remember reading this book and thinking how wrong it was for the government to be snooping (Big Brother) on its citizens. Get used to it! It's happening now! The Big Brother concern is all part of controlling YOU. The Patriot Act should have been called the Big Brother Act.

The picture and words emanating from the television are controlled by forces only *they* want you to see and hear. Remember that nice organization called the Council on Foreign Relations (CFR)? Remember their members supposedly formulate world economic policies and cooperation between nations? The majority of major media companies in the U.S. are members of the CFR.

Say that again? In my opinion, we, the common folk only see half of what is going on and the other half is misrepresentation. And it's done by design to keep the herd (*sheeple*) together and going in one direction, funneling us on a path of continued enslavement and oblivion.

Ever heard of the New World Order? I'm not talking about a pro-wrestling program, but a state of dominating people in all aspects of life and death. It should be called the New World Odor! The smell will knock you over. The scope of this book can't go into detail about the forces behind the NWO, but there's a plethora of information out there that you should research to make your own decision. I feel something is in the wind and I hope I'm long gone before it happens. My concern is about future generations. If this New World Order becomes a reality, it looks bleak for anyone who believes in individual rights.

How does the FED come into play in the scheme of things? What is the big picture? I believe the financial meltdown of 2008 was just a ploy by the powerful few to stick a knife into the back of the American people and hasten the downfall of

POWER OF THE CENTRAL BANK
ARTIST DAVID DEES

this great country. The United States is a beacon for freedom and individual rights throughout the world and therefore is a huge stumbling block for the rich and powerful to take complete control of the world. The Federal Reserve is just a small hand of a bigger arm that governs the program in play for world domination. The powerful few can't take us down militarily, but can wreak havoc financially, ultimately, taking complete control over the United States of America.

The United States can't continue on the same road. We need to travel another road if we are going to survive the attacks on our sovereignty. I said that the United States lost its sovereignty when FDR sold out to the international bankers 1933. I feel we still can make headway against the powerful forces that want to destroy this country.

Albert Einstein once said, *"Insanity: Doing the same thing over and over again and expecting different results."*

We are facing terrible times if we don't change how we make our money. What we need is another Great Awakening! We have trillions of dollars in National Debt and rising by the second. What are we going to do about it? Forget about balancing the budget and raising the debt ceiling and all of those fancy economic ploys our politicians want to do. The only way that we are going to stop the insanity and right the ship is to abolish the Federal Reserve Banking System and start creating our own money. This needs to happen or we are doomed.

"Those who cannot remember the past are condemned to repeat it."

-George Santayana
The Life of Reason, Vol. 1, 1905

A common paraphrase of the above quote is "Those who fail to learn from the mistakes of their predecessors are destined to repeat them." Mr. Santayana, Thomas Jefferson, Andrew Jackson and Abraham Lincoln all understood the evils of central banking. Now the international central bankers are working together to enslave the entire world. When are "We the People" going to learn from history? Having private bankers control our money supply is dead wrong and a detriment to all people who love freedom. Have we crossed the line of no return? Can we do something to stop the madness and save this country from the evil clutches of the powerful few? My answer is a resounding, YES.

Bullet Points to Remember

- know that the media only tells you what the powerful few want you to know

- the Council on Foreign Affairs is very influential on affecting world political and economic policy

- the New World Order is more of a reality than a hoax

- the U.S is being attacked from within and from abroad; the easiest way is to break down the country financially, with the ultimate goal of controlling the United States

- the FED is just a small part of the big picture

<u>Key Questions to Ponder</u>

1. What examples can you give that are distractions to the real problems facing this nation and the world?

2. What does the CFR have to do with the United States and the world in general?

3. What are the key factors in preventing the international bankers from having their way and ruling the world?

4. What do we have to do to help get this country back on track?

5. Is a New World Order on our doorsteps?

"This country, with its institutions, belongs to the people who inhabit it."

Abraham Lincoln, 16th U.S. President
First Inaugural Address, March 4, 1861

"The people are the rightful masters of both congresses and courts—not to overthrow the Constitution, but to overthrow the men *who pervert it."*

-Abraham Lincoln, September 16 & 17, 1859
From notes for speeches in Kansas & Ohio

IX. What Can Be Done, or Is It Too Late?

Our situation is not hopeless, but you need to get fired up and say "Enough is Enough, I'm not taking it anymore!"

The U.S. Constitution, Article I, Section 8, specifically states that Congress has the power

"To coin money, regulate the value thereof, and of foreign coin and fix the standard of weights and measures."

Interesting, the very next sentence in our Constitution says that Congress *"is to provide for the punishment of counterfeiting the securities and current coin of the United States."* In colonial times, counterfeiting paper money was punishable by death as stated on Colonial Scrip. FED officials should have their feet held to the fire for making all of this fake, worthless money. Counterfeiting? They do it every time they push the button to make their fake money out of nothing.

> FED officials should have their feet held to the fire for making all of this fake, worthless money.

If Ben Franklin and Tom Jefferson were sitting around a campfire discussing the exploits of the present-day United States, they would both abolish the Federal Reserve on its blatant unconstitutionality. Greenbacks were bills of credit that Lincoln and the government created to fund the Civil War. Lincoln's simple legislative procedure bypassed the greedy bankers. We need to do that again. Simply, create our own money without having to go to private bankers. The FED every day just pushes a computer key and PRESTO, instant paper bills of credit are produced by the Bureau of Engraving (BEP). For every printed dollar we pay interest on and go into debt. What a racket!! Would you like to put an end to this sham? Here's what you can do:

> You are increasing your knowledge by reading this book.

1. Get educated:
   Knowledge=Power –
   supplement your reading with other books on the subject (see bibliography) – but let me caution you – *Knowledge without Action is APATHY!*

2. Talk to your family and friends - use social networks to spread the word on how corrupt and deceitful the FED is - use the knowledge that you have learned from this book and others.

3. Petition your Congressman to abolish the FED – if more and more people let their wishes be known, maybe

something good would happen – we have the numbers – use them. (See appendix for Form Letter).

4. Write letters to the editor of your local newspaper - talk to groups and civic organizations - get the word out - you may use anything in this book to get your point across.

What can specifically be done now to get rid of the Federal Reserve and restore an honest money system?

1. The U.S. government should buy back the Federal Reserve Banking System - this will take the power away from them and put it back into the hands of the people.

2. *Any interest produced by Treasury instruments i.e. bonds, notes and bills should be re-cycled back into the U.S. Treasury.*

3. *No behind the scenes, under the table dealings, secret meetings etc. – everything that encompasses the nation's money supply will be done in the open and on review by Congress or 3rd party.*

4. *No excess funds given to banks to prop up their fractional reserves - any monies loaned to member banks will be paid back in interest to the U.S. Treasury - the principle from these loans will be constantly re-cycled and used for other bank loans imagine the amount of money from these interest payments and how that would result in extra revenue for Uncle Sam.*

5. *Our Treasury should print and issue all the money in circulation.*

This is just the beginning. By taking control of the money supply away from private bankers, it will allow our government to operate under more favorable conditions and parameters and would give the upper hand on money matters back to the people and maybe, just maybe save this country!

Understand we are dealing with some very powerful people who have our politicians and the media under lock and key. Remember, with knowledge we have the power to change the status quo. If your Congress person bows down to the FED, then don't re-elect them. Easier said than done, but it's a start.

You've been given the gun, I've provided the ammunition. The target is whether you want to continue to live as a slave to the powerful central bankers OR do you want to live in freedom.

Otherwise, you behold to their whims of controlling your money and causing economic turmoil in the form of Busts and Booms. It's your choice!

"The world is in greater peril from those who tolerate or encourage evil than from those who actually commit it."

Albert Einstein's Tribute to Pablo Casals
March 30, 1953

"Those who have the privilege to know, have the duty to act."

Attributed to Albert Einstein by Mike Kirchubel
in his book "Vile Acts of Evil" page 260

Certainly, great words from Mr. Einstein. He knew about physics, but he also had good insight on human nature and this world. I might add to his words, **"If you don't act, then you deserve what you get!"**

Bullet Points to Remember

- -the U.S. Constitution gives power to the Congress to coin money

- -read Article I, Section 8 of the U.S. Constitution

- The FED counterfeits money every day, an act that was a crime punishable by death in colonial America

Key Questions to Ponder

1. What can be done immediately to reduce the power of the Federal Reserve?

2. What can we do as individuals to help abolish the Federal Reserve Banking System?

3. What do Americans have on their side to make changes in their money system?

"Where the people fear the government you have Tyranny. Where the government fears the people you have Freedom."

-John Basil Barnhill, 1914 Debate on Socialism, published in the National Rip-Saw, page 34

X. Final Words . . .
A Financial Armageddon?

The above quote contains simple words, yet they ring so true. Are the people of the United States afraid of their government? I feel that many of us gave up hope and now just plod along like life's the way it's supposed to be. I see more indifference than ever in my travels around the United States.

It's not fear that is turning this country into tyranny, but *apathy* – giving up hope for a better future. When people ask me what they can do to take back this country or change it, I tell them to get EDUCATED. The answers are in front of you, waiting to be discovered and seen.

Seek out independent sources. Do your own research. The main media resides in collusion with the central bankers, the investment bankers on Wall Street and our politicians. I feel the last true President was John F. Kennedy. I believe he stood up for what he believed in and was taken out for his beliefs.

We all have our favorite president, but understand that they are just puppets/robots, put into office to further the agenda of the international bankers and powerful few, including our Federal Reserve. Once you understand this important point, you can start making in-roads at discovering the truth. Look deep enough; the truth will hit you in the face.

> The Federal Reserve needs to be dismantled or we are headed for some horrific outcomes that will change us and future generations.

We need definitive action. Despite the many words written about our problematic economy, I believe I have found what's basically wrong with our country's money supply. More importantly, there's something askew with the psyche of the American people. There are too many distractions and we must to start focusing on the important issues facing this nation or we are going down big time. As citizens of this great nation, we need to feed our spirituality. The hunger is evident in the way we treat our fellow human beings and the greed that is pulling this country apart. Stop the Texting, put down your Phones, stop singing to American Idol, dancing

DAVID DEES

to the Stars and turn off the Housewives – your country is losing its direction, freedom and sovereignty!

We need to come to grips with what is the main cause of the demise of this great nation. The Federal Reserve needs to be dismantled or we are headed for some horrific outcomes that will change us and future generations.

Have you looked at your savings accounts and retirement funds lately? If your retirement fund is looking better, it's just a matter of time before it starts looking worse. Have you noticed no matter how hard you work; you never seem to get ahead of the curve? Our National Debt has reached astronomical proportions and grows larger by the second. There's a reason for that and it starts with our central bank, the Federal Reserve. They are breaking our backs. When I see and hear all of this money being thrown around in the form of bank bailouts, stimulus packages and the Federal government taking over private business, I begin to wonder, are the American people asleep at the wheel?

> This nation is careening at high speed, out of control, without a driver. A ninety degree cliff looms in the distance, waiting to swallow the sovereignty of the United States.

Plain and simple, Crony Capitalism or Fascism is corrupt and evil. Americans are being raked over the coals and don't even know it.

I've handed you a synopsis on what money is and how money has been used throughout history. We talked about how this country came into being and what our Founding Fathers had to say about a central bank. We wondered together why our early politicians voted for "Banks of the United States" and we talked about the men who were vehemently opposed to central banks. The Civil War had little to do with slavery and more to do with the Money Powers. We then discussed the "Beast" and its voracious appetite for our money, leading to what is happening today and what could possibly happen in the future. I've quoted several famous and influential people who know a thing or two about human nature, from Thomas Jefferson to John Steinbeck, and all have come out against the banking demons. If that isn't proof enough, what else do I have to do to convince you?

In my dealings with people, when the topic of discussion turns to the Federal Reserve, most Americans are clueless. Most people accept the FED as an indispensable institution, taking care of our money supply and controlling inflation. But history has proven that they have done nothing but cause major meltdowns and turmoil in our financial system, beginning with the Farm Depression of 1920-21, The Crash of 1929, followed by the Great Depression, our current mess AND lots of mayhem in-between!

I hope you take the information gleaned from these pages and apply it. The American people need to act now. Time is running out. If we desire to have a United States, now and for future generations, that is free and a defender of the human rights of people worldwide, then we need to take notice and start changing things for the better.

I believe both parties have done great harm to the American people. I'm neither Democrat nor Republican or a Third Party person. But I am a *free thinker*. It is my hope a bit of that free thinking style rubs off on YOU!

"Washington's reckless spending spree of the past several years and unwillingness to confront the mountains of debt coming soon from unreformed federal entitlement programs threaten the economic and social future of the generation currently between the ages of 5 and 30.

The 115 million Americans in this Debt-Paying Generation could experience enormous adverse effects from having to pay down the greatest debt in world history. Indeed, those of you in the Debt-Paying Generation could end your working lives as the least improved generation (in U.S. history) relative to the one that preceded you. "

-The Heritage Foundation,
"Slay The Beast: How You Can Save Us from The Massive Debt," William Beach and Rob Bluey, September 28, 2010

Where do you think all of the debt money comes from? It is important that our young people become knowledgeable and understand what the Federal Reserve, in collusion with our politicians have done to the American people. I hope our young people will get a hold of this book, read it from cover to cover and take definitive action. They are the ones that will have to deal with the problems facing this nation, the coming inflation and loss of freedoms.

"Freedom is never more than one generation away from extinction"

-Ronald Reagan, 40th U.S. President
Address to the annual meeting of the
Phoenix Chamber of Commerce, March 30, 1961
Also CA Gubernatorial Inauguration Speech, Jan. 5, 1967

This nation is careening at high speed, out of control, without a driver. A ninety degree cliff looms in the distance, waiting to swallow the sovereignty of the United States.

Only WE can stop it.

Get empowered, learn and take action.

"The bank is something more than men, I tell you. It's the monster. Men made it, but they can't control it."

-John Steinbeck, <u>The Grapes of Wrath</u>, Chapter 5

I believe that we can control it. We need to throw out the Money Changers like Jesus did in Matthew's parable. Are you up to the task?

"Whoever trusts in his riches will fail, but the righteous will thrive like a green leaf"

-Proverbs 11:28

I started this book with an indictment against the Federal Reserve Banking System. I have presented the evidence: GUILTY OR NOT GUILTY? What is your verdict?

Furthermore, is the FED a viable institution or a hindrance to the sovereignty and goodness of the United States of America?

"The banks – commercial banks and the Federal Reserve – create all the money of this nation and its people pay interest on every dollar of that newly created money. Which means that private banks exercise unconstitutionally, immorally, and ridiculously the power to tax the people. For every newly created dollar dilutes to some extent the value of every other dollar already in circulation.

This is the very heart of inflation. It is also taxation without representation with a vengeance. Until this system is changed, our debt will continue to skyrocket without limit and the fixing of debt limits by the Congress will continue to be an exercise in utter futility.

U.S. Representative, Jerry Voorhis, (D-CA) 1937 - 1947,
<u>Beyond Victory</u>, 1944

XI. Selected Readings

The following are some thoughts and writings of others who feel the Federal Reserve has ruined the sovereignty of this great country by their monetary policies and hidden agendas. I'm not the only one who thinks this country would be in better shape if we didn't have a private central bank controlling our money.

From Texas Congressman Ron Paul's book, END the FED:

Why END the FED?, page 141

The Federal Reserve should be abolished because it is immoral, unconstitutional, impractical, promotes bad economics and undermines liberty. Its destructive nature makes it a tool of tyrannical government.

Nothing good can come from the Federal Reserve. It is the biggest taxer of them all. Diluting the value of the dollar by increasing its supply is a vicious, sinister tax on the poor and middle class.

The Federal Reserve's monetary policy has brought us to where we are today—in a tragic economic mess. Though the dollar survives for now, the international financial system built over the past thirty-eight years has been brought down by market forces. The fiat dollar reserve standard that evolved out of the breakdown of Bretton Woods in 1971 has come to an end. That is the significance of the economic crisis in which we find ourselves.

Central Banks and Wars, page 63

Following the creation of the FED, the government would discover other uses for an elastic money supply aside from keeping the banking system from defaulting on its obligations. It would prove useful in funding war. It is no coincidence that the century of total war coincided with the century of central banking. When governments had to fund their own wars without a paper money machine to rely upon, they economized on resources. They found diplomatic solutions to prevent war, and after they started a war they ended it as soon as possible.

From author, Michael Kirchubel's book, <u>VILE ACTS of EVIL</u>:

How Banks Make Money, 242

Under the Federal Reserve System . . . the bankers know a good thing (for them) when they see it and they are not about to let go of their money making machine, no matter what the cost to the rest of us . . . we taxpayers will never be able to pay off our National Debt and will continue to pay bankers hard interest on money they create out of thin air, forever.

Parting Thoughts, page 438

As the fisherman casts his net and then pulls it back, the economic elite of this world expand our money supply and then contract. With every cycle they pocket our property, earnings and dreams. They charge us interest on every dollar in circulation every minute of every day. They buy laws, lawyers, lobbyists and legislators to make their criminal action "legal" and they control the media to keep us unaware. But now you know.

From Ronald MacDonald and Robert Rowen, M.D. book, THE OWN IT ALL (Including YOU!):

Epilogue, page 185

The whole financial system since 1933 is a fraudulent balloon, a creation of the Bea$t. Pundits are calling for honest "reform," admitting decades of mismanagement. But few are looking at the truth. We have been denied our unalienable rights and allowed our government to rob and steal for the benefit of the Bea$t, represented by the international bankers. The real mismanagement is "currency of theft" (liened FRNs). The real problem is not **"toxic"** *mortgages as the government is leading you to believe. The fundamental problem is* **"toxic"** *currency, which underlies* **all** *of the problems. We could have never had* **"toxic mortgages"** *had we been lent substance (honest money) instead of toxic currency (fraud/illusion), which is based on debt. Illusion, like a desert mirage, disappears. Gold/substance does not.*

From Charles Goyette's book, THE DOLLAR MELTDOWN:

The Federal Reserve System

The Federal Reserve is central to America's most devastating bubbles and busts, and is responsible for almost a hundred years of criminal scale dollar destruction, page 75 . . . a central bank such as the Federal Reserve represents the politicization of money . . . From its shadowy beginnings, until today the Federal Reserve has been cloaked in secrecy. This secrecy conceals its hidden beneficiaries, and obscures the costs paid by the people, page 76 . . . more alarming is the role of the central bank in funding wars not popular enough to be sustained by direct taxation, pages 76-77 . . . Ninety-six cents of the value of every dollar has vanished on the FED's watch, and we've seen the worst depression and the worst bank failures in the nation's history, massive malfunctions in the credit markets, bubbles and busts, all under the great money and credit engineers of the central bank. It's been a costly affair, the infatuations of nineteenth-century intellectuals notwithstanding, page 81.

From Eustace Clarence Mullins book, <u>A Study of the Federal Reserve and Its Secrets</u>

The Federal Reserve Act as signed by Woodrow Wilson contained no stabilization mechanism, but did contain plenty of factors which would make stabilization impossible. Its manipulation of the discount rate to vary the amount of money in circulation, and its open market operations, dumping quantities of Government securities on the New York Exchange or withholding then to create credit expansion or contraction, were the conditions directly responsible for the greatest disaster this country has ever suffered, The Great Depression of 1929-31.

XII. OTHER TOPICS

1. THE GOLD STANDARD

The Gold Standard is a monetary system in which the standard economic unit of account is a fixed weight of gold.

Having our money backed by something of value (intrinsic), like precious metals, would instill honesty into our money system.

The Federal Reserve is basically the "Bank of Congress" and anytime our politicians want to fund their pet projects, they go to the FED, float Treasury bills and the FED hands them money created by a computer keystroke. How easy and convenient for Congress to have a privately owned bank always ready to "lend" money at interest at the expense of the American taxpayer.

A Gold Monetary System (GMS) would not only stop the illicit collusion of politicians with central bankers, but would stop the "moral hazard" associated with investment banks. These banks would think twice before putting their money into risky investments, knowing that if they lose, it's not a simple paper loss, but a loss of hard, honest money. Banks, in general, would be held to a higher standard and would be careful how they allocate assets. Banks who practiced poor business would fail, while others with strong business models would flourish. The free market would dictate what banks survive and who falls by the wayside – not the government and this "To Big To Fail" mentality.

Advantages of GMS

1. Long-term price stability
2. Promotes economic prosperity
3. Check on deficit spending
4. Helps savers by preventing money from being devalued or destroyed by inflation
5. Eliminates Boom & Bust cycles because of inelastic money supply
6. Difficult to manipulate
7. Eliminates the "borrowing" of fake, fiat money from central bankers and allows the government to create its own money backed by intrinsic value and substance

Some economists dislike a GMS and I admit there are some inherent problems, but the current system is not working and either needs to be abolished or re-tuned drastically.

What bothers me is that we can discover new cures for cancer and put men on the moon, but can't devise an honest money system that benefits all people. Returning to a GMS would take the power out of the hands of the central bankers and politicians and put it back where it belongs with the people. A measured unit of gold is gold and can only be manipulated by man. Above all, we need HONESTY in our money and a GMS would do that.

2. THE PURPOSE/FUNCTION OF THE FEDERAL RESERVE

Author's Note: I've placed + or − sign after each function to indicate the FED's failure/success in accomplishing its purposes. All of the following information is taken from the Federal Reserve's website, except the bold comments.

1. To address the problem of banking panics (-) **they cause bank panics**

2. To serve as a central bank for the United States (+)

3. To strike a balance between private interests of banks and the centralized responsibility of government (-) **there's no balance, only collusion between the FED and the U.S. government**

   a. to supervise and regulate banking institutions (-) **no supervision or regulation**

   b. to protect credit rights of consumers (-) **miserable failure in this area**

4. To manage the nation's money supply through monetary policy to achieve the sometimes conflicting goals of

   a. maximum employment (-) **we have high unemployment**

   b. stable prices, including prevention of either inflation or deflation (-) – **inflation has always been a problem**

   c. moderate long-term interest rates (-) **only at the FED's convenience**

5. To maintain the stability of the financial system and contain systemic risk in financial markets (-) **FED's monetary policies have made our financial systems worse**

6. To provide financial services to depository institutions, the U.S. government, and foreign official institutions, including playing a major role in operating the nation's payments system

   a. to facilitate the exchange of payments among regions (+)
   b. to respond to local liquidity needs (+)

7. To strengthen U.S. standing in the world economy (-) **has only weakened U.S. since 1913**

Let's see: 9 negatives and 3 positives – to me, the Federal Reserve is a PATHETIC FAILURE in its Purpose and Functions.

3. THE FEDERAL RESERVE AND POLITICS

In my opinion, the U.S. political landscape is bleak. It's like a worn-out engine in a clapped out car – the body of the car is rusty and old; the engine sputters and spurts, while the car sits and goes nowhere.

Do you think anything will change if either Obama or Romney is elected to office? I have difficulty with both candidates and how they relate to the Money Power in this country. Obama is a socialist, while Romney caters to the corporate elite. I do feel that Obama is leading the United States down the path of a socialistic, European model of government. A direction I would not want to travel. This does not bode well for our country's sovereignty, individual rights and freedom. In this regard,

Romney is the better choice. Understand, the international bankers, including our Federal Reserve love socialism. Without a central bank's collusion with the state, socialism could not exist.

"If one understands that socialism is not a share-the-wealth program, but is in reality a method to consolidate and control the wealth, then the seeming paradox of super-rich men promoting socialism becomes no paradox at all. Instead, it becomes logical, even the perfect tool of power-seeking megalomaniacs. Communism or more accurately, socialism, is not a movement of the downtrodden masses, but of the economic elite."

-Gary Allen, <u>None Dare Call It Conspiracy</u>, 1971, page 32

Based on the above quote, are the central banks of the world, including our own, conspiring to enslave the masses of the world in a socialistic web of discontent and misery? Are we turning to the socialism/communism of the defunct Soviet Union? Could this be the plan? Is there a New World Order – one government, one currency looking us in the eye?

This brings to mind one of my favorite musical plays entitled, *1776*, when Founding Father John Adams implores his fellow patriots on what he envisions for the new United States of America. He sings:

Is anybody here?
Does anybody care?
Does anyone see what I see?

I believe our presidential elections and the candidates who are running; including our sitting President is an affront to the

American people. The candidates are puppets to the Money Power and the election process is a ploy to deceive and distract us from the real issue on how the power elites control us.

It doesn't matter who is elected. Our politicians are married to the cheap, easy money provided by the Federal Reserve and nothing will change until we demand the abolishment of the illegal collusion between our government and the FED.

Opinions abound on the above subject. The fact is that the Federal Reserve thrives on a state supported, welfare-socialistic-fascists agenda. The more fake money they produce, the more goes into their greedy pockets. The more money they have, the more control they exert over us.

Do some research on the *Amero* (WorldNet Daily, Dec. 13, 2006). Similar to the Euro, this unit of money is already on the books. Once our dollar fails, the *Amero* will go into place as a currency for Canada, the United States and Mexico. The globalist's banksters are pushing for no borders, collectivism, totalitarianism and one currency that will fit their needs to keep us subservient and under CONTROL.

Go to <u>You Tube</u> and view *<u>The Day the Dollar Collapses</u>* for an eye-opening scenario on what happens once the U.S. dollar fails and is no longer accepted as the world's currency. It's scary and happening right before our eyes!

Does anyone see what I see?

4. REASONS TO ABOLISH FEDERAL RESERVE

a. -It's UNCONSTITUTIONAL
b. -It clearly fails in its stated purpose and functions (see above)
c. -It is operated by private bankers controlling public money
d. -It's lack of transparency and secrecy is detrimental to the People's rights and freedoms guaranteed by the U.S. Constitution
e. -It fosters and supports wars
f. -It encourages Totalitarianism and Plutocracy
g. -Through debasing of the U.S. dollar, it causes inflation and levels an unfair hidden tax on the middle class
h. -Through its illicit monetary policies it destabilizes the U.S. economy

5. THE ROTHSCHILDS

A discussion about the Federal Reserve and central banking would not be complete without saying a few words about the Rothschilds.

The House of Rothschild began in the middle seventeenth century by Mayer Amschel Bauer, the son of a goldsmith from Frankfurt, Germany. Mayer had five sons, and changed his last name to Rothschild, basing his name on the German words meaning *"Red Shield,"* which became their business logo. Through the practice of perfecting fractional banking, the Rothschilds acquired a huge fortune. As the family prosperity increased, Mayer sent his five sons to other major European cities to establish banking practices. The Rothschild brothers using their money and influence invested and conducted transactions on behalf of many European governments and monarchs in the 18th century. The brothers found special court and ran the central banks of Germany, Austria, Italy, France and England. The Rothschild name became known throughout Europe. They used their wealth and connections to influence politics and wars.

From the establishment of the Bank of England in 1694 to Napoleon's defeat at Waterloo in 1815, England was at war for 63 of those years (over half) – the other years were spent preparing for war. The English central bankers, with Nathan Rothschild at the helm, had a hand in fostering some of these wars and keeping their pockets filled with blood money.

"As mentioned, by the early 1800's, the five Rothschild sons controlled the central banks, and thus the finances, and thus the governments of Germany, France, Italy, England and Austria. Their control was absolute."

<u>Vile Acts of Evil</u>, Michael Kirchubel, page 41

The Rothchilds had an iron grip on the finances of Europe and used their money power to control governments and monarchies, often, instigating wars and social change to enrich their banking dynasty. What is interesting, nothing is ever mentioned in history books about their effects on nations or the banking industry. Even today their name is hardly mentioned in the news. I wonder why?

"For the last hundred and fifty years, the history of the House of Rothschild has been to an amazing extent the backstage history

of Western Europe . . . Because of their success in making loans not to individuals, but to nations, they reaped huge profits . . . Someone once said that the wealth of Rothschilds consists of the bankruptcy of nations."

-Fredric Morton, The Rothschilds, 1961
As quoted in Eustace Mullins' book The Secrets of the Federal
Reserve, Chapter 5

"The Rothschilds can start or prevent wars. Their word could make or break empires."

-Chicago Evening American Newspaper, December 3, 1923

The above quote is from 1923, ten years after the inception of the Federal Reserve. Do you think the Rothschilds had any influence in our central bank's policies in the 1920's? Did they mitigate the 1929 Market Crash that put the United States into The Great Depression and Germany on the road to war? How about FDR's confiscation of gold from the people of the United States?

Even today the Rothschild sphere of influence is felt in our financial markets. The large investment bank, JP Morgan Chase, is a direct descendent of the House of Rothschild. The Red Shield is missing from the JP Morgan Chase logo, but the power to control and deceive is very prevalent, as evidenced by their recent loss of two billion in investment dollars.

How can a few wealthy individuals control the world? The Rothschilds did it and are still doing it today from behind the closed curtains.

6. HOW THE FED PRODUCES MONEY

Our money begins with a fancy designed piece of paper "inked" by our government called a Treasury bond or note (an instrument of government debt). The Federal Reserve "buys" the bond or note and marks it as an asset in their books. In turn, another piece of paper is printed in the form of a Federal Reserve Check that totals the amount of the bond or note. Keep in mind that the FED doesn't have any account to cover this check – in essence, this money is created out of nothing. Incredulously, the FED charges interest on this Federal Reserve Check. This check is deposited into a government account and used to pay government expenses. Government checks are cut to employers and the first wave of fake money hits the economy. Some people deposit these checks into their banks, but instead of being a liability, the banks mark them down as assets (reserves) and lends this money out as loans to other bank customers (fractional banking).

Let's put some numbers on the above. Let's say the U.S. Government needs money and comes to the Federal Reserve with one of those fancy bonds for $1,000.00. The FED takes that bond and magically out of thin air turns it into a $1,000.00 Federal Reserve Check and charges interest on it. The $1,000.00 FED check is deposited in a government account to pay expenses. The people receiving these payments deposit their money into their respective banks. Let's say John Q Public received that $1,000.00. Public's *All Fair Bank* takes his $1,000.00 and marks it on the ledger as an asset and lends it out to another customer, while charging interest on that loan. The bank only has to keep 10% of it in reserve and now has $900 to lend out. Just like the Federal Reserve, the bank has created money out of nothing and charged interest on it. The beat goes on and on!

In G. Edward Griffin's book, *The Creature from Jekyll Island*, Mr. Griffin goes into detail how our money is produced by the FED and how it is multiplied over and over again.

Just understand that our money is made from DEBT and created out of NOTHING – both deleterious to the general welfare of "We the People." Now you understand why this nation is facing a National Debt into the trillions.

7. FORMER REP. GRAYSON (FLORIDA) VERSUS FED CHAIRMAN BEN BERNANKE (YOU TUBE)

If you want to see first hand the deceit and corruption emanating from the Federal Reserve, go to You Tube and view the 2-3 minute video clip of the verbal exchange between Rep. Grayson and Chairman of the Federal Reserve, Ben Bernanke. Grayson didn't last long as a representative from Florida, but he did a nice job of putting Bernanke on the hot seat with his questioning of the FED's budget. Bernanke's words and body language says it all.

8. JIMMY MAC'S HIGH FIVE (HOORAH!!)

In the previous chapter, What Can Be Done, I gave you "cookbook" solutions to ending the domination of private bankers controlling our money. I have my own thoughts on how we can transition into an honest money system that stabilizes the economy and restores the American Dream. My main thrust in restoring confidence in this nation's economy is to remove the "Money Power" from the private bankers. "We the People" need to take back control in how our money is produced. We can do this by performing the following:

1. ABOLISH

First and foremost, would petition Congress to ABOLISH the Federal Reserve. Get the POWER out of their hands. This has to happen first before anything!

2. CREATE

Through a Constitutional Amendment allow the U.S. Government to start CREATING its own money/bills of credit through the Treasury Department, without paying interest to a third party (Federal Reserve). This act would be similar to when Lincoln printed Greenbacks to support the Civil War.

3. ELECT

Elect by popular vote a representative (possibly economists from academia) from each of the 12 current Federal Reserve districts, with corresponding elected Advisory Council (6-8 members representing different factions of the economy); this Council would have a single-minded attack on solving problems with our monetary system; this council would meet once a month and report directly to their representative; each month the 12 representatives from the districts would meet to discuss and formulate U.S. monetary policy depending on economic conditions; bankers and politicians would not be allowed as representatives (conflict of interest), but would be permitted to serve on Advisory Councils; there would be staggered terms of service so that new people and ideas would be brought to the forefront on a regular basis.

4. TRANSPARENCY and ACCOUNTABILITY

Not only demand Transparency and Accountability, but give proof and present to the people on a regular basis.

5. HONEST MONEY

Eventually, in 1-3 years, transition to a Gold Standard Monetary System.

The above steps are not the end, but the beginning of removing the POWER from the hands of the connected, rich central bankers and stopping the illegal collusion between the FED, Wall Street and Congress. It's a start! A lot of work needs to be done and it will not be easy. We can't continue down the same path. If we don't change the status quo soon, a financial Armageddon, coupled with a globalist banker takeover is heading our way.

9. HOME-GROWN SCRIPT
(REMEMBER COLONIAL SCRIP?)

These examples show that we do have other alternatives to FRN's (Federal Reserve Notes).

Some Baltimore-area residents were discussing the economic crisis in early 2010, according to Jeff Dicken, director of BGCA (Baltimore Green Currency Association). "We figured that the most effective thing we could do in order to create local economic opportunity and reclaim some of the power that had been stolen by the big banks and corporations would be to start a city-wide currency for Baltimore," Dicken said.

A $10 Federal Reserve note can be exchanged for 11 Bnotes which then trade equal with FRN's at participating merchants.

In Traverse City, Michigan, in 2005, "Bay Bucks" were offered in denominations of 1, 5, 10 and 20 Bay Bucks. These paper script notes were equal to FRN's and accepted as such by participating merchants and businesses.

You might ask is this legal under U.S law? Yes, as long as the issued script follows certain guidelines established by the U.S. Treasury Department. For example, script cannot be redeemable in fake FRN's, only in merchandise.

The above is just an example of how we can by pass the debt-laden FRN's and produce our own money as a medium of exchange.

10. COMING ATTRACTIONS?
(WORSE CASE SCENARIO)

The United States has a major financial meltdown and the international central bankers (World Bank & IMF) intervene with big smiles, cigars and pats on our backs and say that they will save us and the day. The Federal Reserve is eliminated and the World Bank institutes a monetary system with the Amero (see above) as the main medium of exchange. This action essentially takes over the United States money system under the auspices of foreign bankers. What appears to be a friendly gesture by the international bankers in reality is a ploy to take control of our money AND the United States of America.

You say the above can't happen? It's now happening in Europe. Greece might still be Greek, but it's beholding to the World Bank and the IMF for its financial health and welfare.

Folks, if we don't take care of business here in the United States by taking down the Money Power, the above scenario will be playing on your main screen in your living room very soon.

XIII. Epilogue

THE LEAP . . . !!

Like a gourmet dinner, I hope this book has provided savory appetizers and a bountiful main course, digested with tasty drinks to accent the meal's flavor. Upset stomach? Knowing how the Federal Reserve uses your money against you should make you quite queasy and uneasy. But wait, I've saved the best for last. I've prepared a very special dessert, which will sweeten all that you have garnered from these pages and bring you full circle. Sit back, relax and digest. We all need a little sugar in our life!

Some naysayers see dark storm clouds brewing on the horizon for the United States of America. Others say that we have lost our spiritual and moral compass and will implode. In these unsettling and stormy times, I do see a small white cloud clamoring for our attention. As Americans, we need to re-discover the moral and spiritual character our Founding Fathers intended for this country. We do this through His word, the *Bible*. Whether you believe or not, this nation has been "blessed" with an overabundance of wealth. Look around you – it's all in front of your eyes. As people, we are squandering these riches on a crooked path, with *greed* on one side and *apathy* on the other. Our Founding Fathers had a better plan. We need to take the crooks out of the path and start walking collectively on the straight and narrow. It's imperative that the *Bible* becomes a best-seller again or this country will perish as Rome did over 1300 years ago.

"...the Bible offers a moral code as the spinal column of

morality. Most of the world's misery and the problems of society, the family and the individual, may be attributed to the fact that humanity has neglected this spinal column of morality: God's law."

-David Marshall, *Experiencing the Power of the Word*, 1999, page 28

There's a book that I read a few years ago entitled, <u>The Five Thousand Year Leap</u>. I would highly recommend every American read this book. It gives you insight on the ideas and principles this country was founded on. What many Americans forget is that the United States of America, as envisioned by our Founding Fathers, is a special country with a unique governing system of checks and balances with Executive, Legislative and Judicial branches of government. This country is an experiment that is still in the making and evolving, but unfortunately, failing in its purpose. As people, we have lost the "God" in our country. Our Founding Fathers gave us fertile fields to plow, filled with God's bounty. This acreage is now choked with weeds and needs to be cleared of the pestilence and re-planted again. God must be brought back to the consciousness of Americans, especially our lawmakers and shapers of policy, not to exclude CEOs of large corporations such as banks, insurance companies, investment firms and the media.

Our early politicians were guided by *Divine Providence*. They went on to say that our Creator endowed us with unalienable rights and freedoms protected by our Constitution and Bill of Rights. The *Bible* weighed heavily on our Founding Father's decision to develop a government By the People, For the People and Of the People. They knew from previous governing systems (Monarchies) that people's rights were trampled and secondary to the King's authority and sovereignty. They devised a system where States' Rights trump the limited power of the central government. They understood that if safeguards were not in place, man's natural proclivity for Power and Greed would rule the People and cause untold malfeasance and misery. Similar to what is happening today.

Over the last half century, "We the People" have become complacent and granted our politicians the upper hand. We have allowed the powerful few to control and dominate us. It started in 1962 when we granted favor to the politicians to remove "God" from our schools. Since this epic date, I feel our country has been in a tailspin and could hit rock bottom if fundamental changes are not made.

The pendulum has swung too far and is way out of balance. I believe evil has dominion over the sway of the pendulum. There's a battle raging. To win, we must return to the basics of *Faith, Family and Freedom*. This is the ultimate solution to our country's problems.

"Your eyes are windows of your body. If you open your eyes wide in wonder and belief, your body fills up with light. If you live squinty-eyed in greed and distrust, your body is a dank cellar. If you pull the blinds on your window, what dark life you will have!"

-Matthew, 6:22-23, *The Message,*Eugene Peterson, 2003.

We all need to open our eyes to see the light. Through our Founding Father's God-fearing principles and beliefs, the dark clouds need to be banished from this land. Divine Providence got this country on the map. Divine Providence can bring it back to a prosperous life. But, we must pray. We need to take a giant leap in FAITH!

"Please Lord, deliver us from the evil that threatens and

envelops this great Nation. Through Your Word, bring us back to a place where our Founding Fathers wanted us to be. We pray in God's name, Amen!"

That white cloud looms in the distance. Will it dissipate and give way to the dark or produce more white clouds and a brighter future for all Americans?

God's word is the way out of the wilderness and away from the darkening clouds.

"It's better to live right and be poor than to be sinful and rich. The wicked will lose all of their power, but the Lord gives strength to everyone who is good."

Psalm 37: 16-17

With the grace of God, "We the People" will prevail.

XIV. BIBLIOGRAPHY

1. Griffin, G. Edward. *The Creature from Jekyll Island.* Westlake Village, CA. American Media, 1994

2. Paul, Ron. *End the Fed.* New York, NY. Hachette Book Group, New York, 2009

3. Kirchubel, Michael A. *Vile Acts of Evil Volume 1.* 2009

4. Smith, Craig R. and Lowell Point. *The Inflation Deception,* 2012

5. Mullins, Eustace. A Study of the *Federal Reserve and its Secrets.* Blacksburg, VA., Wilder Publications, 2010

6. Rothbard, Murry N. *The Case Against the Fed.* Auburn, AL. Mises Institute, 1994

7. Mises, Ludwig von. *Causes of the Economic Crisis.* Auburn Al. Mises Institute, 2006

8. Goyette, Charles. *The Dollar Meltdown.* Penguin Group, New York, NY. 2009

9. MacDonald, Ronald and Rowen, Robert. *They Own It All (Including You) by Means of Toxic Currency,* 2009

10. Skousen, Cleon. The Five Thousand Year Leap. National Center for Constitutional Rights, 1981, 7th ed, 2009

All of the above books are excellent resources for you to read to become more familiar with the Federal Reserve. These are books that will supplement what you have read in this book. I would encourage you to do your own research, and come to your own conclusion on whether the FED has been good or bad for this country. I consider Griffin's book, *The Creature from Jekyll Island*, the bible for learning more specific information about the Federal Reserve. His book reads like a history book and it will show you how money has been used for and against man. An excellent read!

JP McCarthy, 2012

XV. INDEX

XVI. APPENDIX

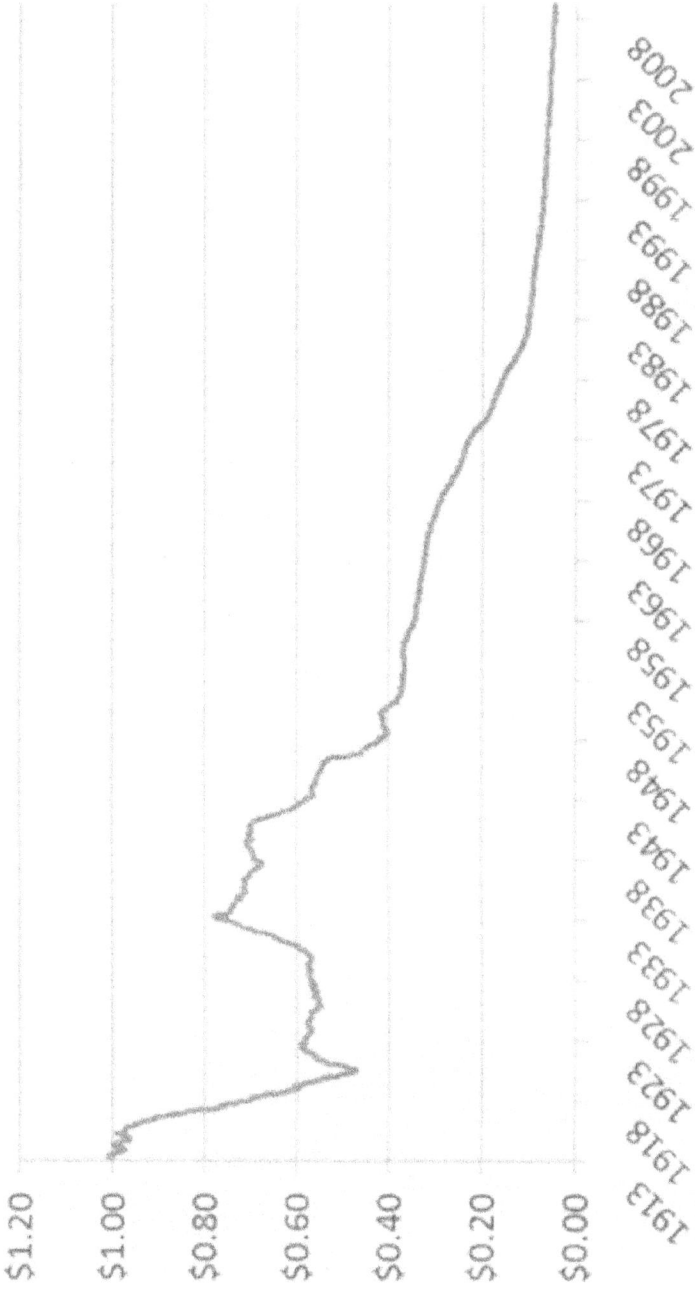

A. Purchasing Power of the U.S. Dollar, January 1913 = $1.00

B.

Purchasing Power in the United States of Gold and Selected Currencies
(1913 = 1.0)

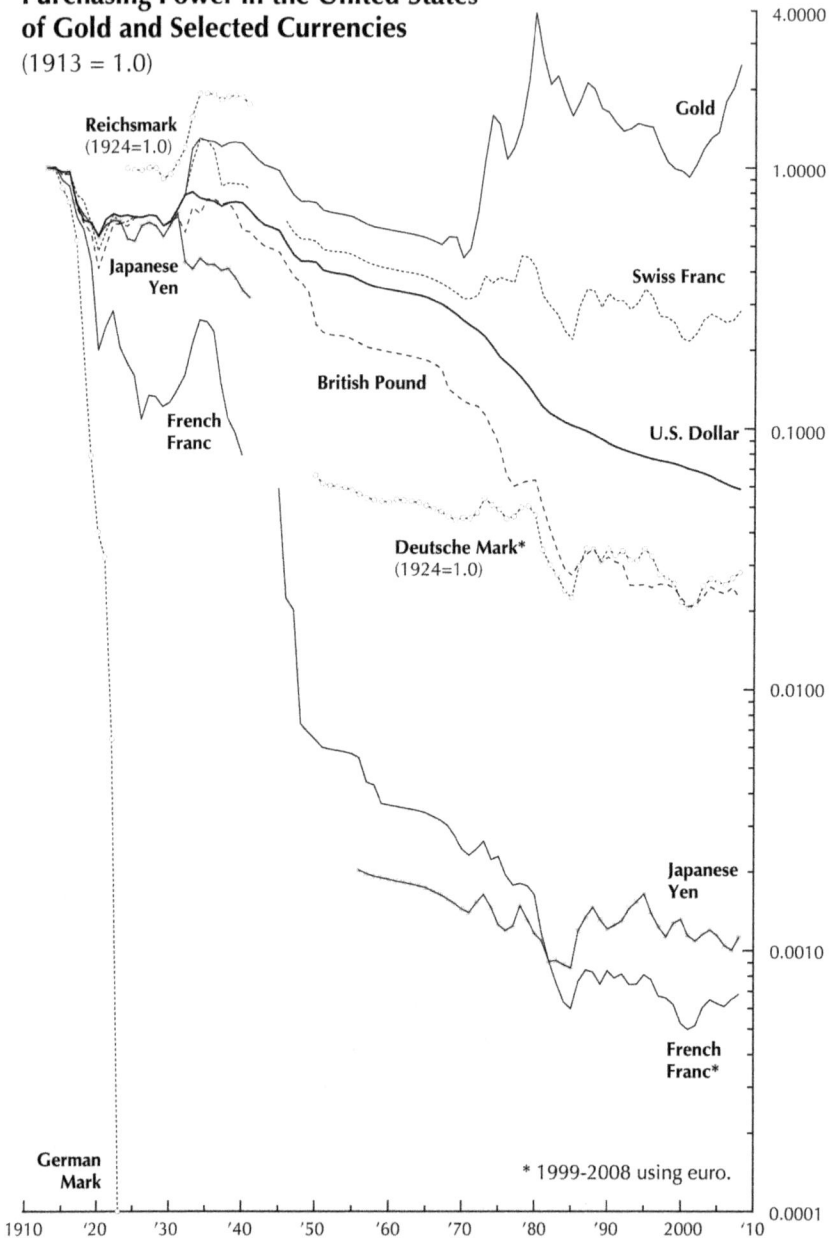

Note: Purchasing power calculated from the implicit price deflator for U.S. GDP and the exchange rates of foreign currencies for U.S. dollars.

C. Booms and Busts in the U.S. Economy since WWII

Just like the ups and downs of a roller coaster are strategically timed, the Fed can impact the ups and downs of our economy. Here is a list of the economic recessions and their causes since 1945.

Feb. – Oct. 1945   Decrease in government spending after WWII.

Nov. '48 – Oct. '49   Veterans returned to workforce, competing for jobs, and causing the unemployment rate to climb to 5.9%.

July '53 – May '54   **The Federal Reserve tightened the money supply** to curb the rising inflation following the Korean War.

Aug. '57 – Apr. '58   **Government tightened monetary policy** to years prior to the recession to curb inflation, but prices continued to rise through 1959. The sharp world-wide recession and the strong U.S. Dollar contributed to a foreign trade deficit.

Apr. '60 – Feb. '61 Americans shifted to buying compact and foreign made cars, and industry drew down inventories.

Dec. '69 – Nov. '70 Increasing inflation caused **the government to employ a very restrictive monetary policy.**

Nov. '73 – Mar. '75 Oil prices quadrupled and high government spending on the Vietnam War. Unemployment reached 9% in May 1975.

Jan. – July 1980 Inflation had reached 13.5% and **the Federal Reserve raised interest rates and slowed money supply growth,** which caused unemployment to rise.

July '81 – Nov. '82 Regime change in Iran, the world's 2nd largest producer of oil at the time. **The government enforced a tighter monetary policy** to control rampant inflation. Prime rate reached 21.5% in 1982.

July '90 – Mar. '91 Iraq invaded Kuwait, which spiked oil prices causing manufacturing to decline. Manufacturing was also being moved offshore, and the United Airlines buyout triggered a stock market crash.

Mar. – Nov. 2001 Collapse of the "dotcom bubble", 911 attacks, and accounting scandals at major U.S. corporations.

2003 Iraqi and Afghanistan Wars

Dec. '07 – Present Sub-prime mortgage crisis, housing bubble bust and collapse of financial institutions.

D. Form Letter to Send to Congress to Abolish the Federal Reserve

DATE: _____

Congress/Man/Woman/Representative_____

It has come to my attention that our Central Bank, the Federal Reserve is unconstitutional based on *Article I, Section 8* of the United States Constitution. When you took office you swore to follow and defend the Constitution. Why do you allow private bankers to have control over our money supply? More importantly, why do you allow the Federal Reserve to exist?

The Federal Reserve through its illicit monetary policies is a detriment to the freedoms guaranteed by our Constitution since its inception in 1913. "We the People" of the United States have suffered long enough and want the illegal collusion between the FED, Wall Street Banks and the U.S. government to stop. It is your duty as my elected representative to restore honesty, integrity and virtue back into our money system. We want our country free from the money power so we as Americans can start creating our own money instead of borrowing it from private bankers at interest.

Sincerely,

About the Author

JP McCarthy was born near
Boston and raised in Maryland.
After graduating from the
University of Maryland Dental
School in 1980, he entered the
military. He did 5 tours of active duty in Iraq with the U.S. Army,
and retired as a Colonel. JP is presently living in Flagler Beach,
Florida.

He has written two other books, one a fiction novel entitled,
Ground Zero and Beyond in 2003, the second a non-fiction work
called, *Vintage Racing-Start to Finish* in 1991. Go to his website:
www.fedruin.com for more information and suggestions on ways
to abolish the Federal Reserve. You may also order additional
copies of *THE MONEY SPIDERS, the Ruin-NATION of the United
States by the Federal Reserve* from this site.

Author's Note: for discounted bulk orders for schools, churches
and other organizations, contact the author or ClearView Press,
Inc. at www.clearviewpressinc.com or 256-867-7468.

NOTES:

www.ingramcontent.com/pod-product-compliance
Lightning Source LLC
Chambersburg PA
CBHW071214020426
42333CB00015B/1405